Daniel Hernández Osorio

To Fail or to Succeed: It's your choice

THE ROAD OF SUCCESS

Publisher
D'har Services
P.O. Box 290
Yelm, WA 98597
www.dharservices.com
info@dharservices.com
dharservices@gmail.com

Cover by Xiomara García

Copyright© 2015 Daniel Hernández Osorio

ISBN-13: 978-1-939948-37-3

All rights reserved.
No part of this book may be reproduced in any form or by any means, including photographic, photocopying, or electronic process or in the form of a phonographic recording; nor may it be stored in a retrieval system, transmitted, or otherwise be copied for public or private use-other than for "fair use" as brief quotations embodied in articles and reviews, without permission in written from the owned author.

Printing in USA

To my fifth son, Arturo, fruit of the love between two hearts and our faith in God. Like an angel sent to us, he has filled our home and lives with much happiness; with his world of fantasy: Merlin, his guard dog; Crown and Birdy, his Burmese cats, who faithfully help him to paint his dreams in the rainbow of the unexpected.

Acknowledgements

First, I would like to thank Angelica Lorenz, my wife, for providing me with her unconditional support, wisdom and patience, as I endeavor to fulfill my dreams.

To Julio Daniel, my eldest son, who has all the qualities of a compassionate and successful human being.

To my daughters, whom I love greatly and with all my heart:

Andrea Carolina, who chose to be a math teacher, I am very proud of you.

*Juldy Roxana, a professional in the field of sports physiology
and psychology, graduated from Florida State University; whose
love and joy are a blessing beyond a doubt, just as she is a blessing to me and to her patients.*

Maria Fernanda, who uses art as the means to express her spirituality, and enjoys teaching that the world needs only be a little more just and simple.

To my four grandchildren, whose tenderness lights my soul:

Juldy Samantha and Eliana, my beautiful granddaughters.

Chris and Sam, my intelligent little ones.

To my parents, Julio Daniel and Marina (RIP), the best parents in the world.

To my brothers and sisters: Hector, Piedad, Analida, Marlen, Elizabeth, Marina, Juldy, Rosangela, Mauricio and Jimmie, thank you for being who you are.

Specially dedicated to Mr. Richard Deeb, whose teachings left an indelible mark in my life. May he rest in the glory of God.

It is the desire in my heart to honor the help I received from all the people who, directly or indirectly, supported me throughout the process of writing this book. To them, I send many blessings.

I would like to emphasize the invaluable collaboration of Catalina Paez Torres, BS. in Service Management, who dedicated much of her time to the task of helping me to organize, select and transcribe much of the information contained in this work.

PROLOGUE

To write the prologue to one of my father's books is a source of internal pride; and to be a part of something that holds great significance for him is a privilege. Therefore, I would like to thank him for choosing me to write this prologue, for being my guide, my friend and for believing in my unlimited abilities.

My father is the person that I respect the most in the world, and the possibility of writing a prologue not worthy of him caused me a lot anxiety, so I must confess I delayed it for a while. At first, because when I began to read the book I found that my subconscious had an aversion to the content in some of its chapters; it was as if in some manner they were contrary to my beliefs. Although I made an effort to read them, I could not manage to do it all the way until the end. For reasons I could not fathom, something continued to prevent me from finishing the book; like an invisible barrier that either made me forget about it, or kept me from having the time to read it. In short, every single time I grabbed the book to read it, something new prevented me from accomplishing my objective.

One day, I finally understood that I was the one who continually put those obstacles in my way: If I really wanted to read it, I would have already done it. I decided to do away with the excuses and finish reading the book; it took me exactly three days to do it, pausing every time I needed in order to ponder about the information I was reading.

I discovered that once I decided to read the book, it all happened at the perfect time. I had the feeling it had been written just for me. The words contained in each page held a message particular to the circumstances of my personal, family, professional, emotional or spiritual life at the moment. I could apply every example on the book to my own life. The fact that it flowed so perfectly made me a little bit concerned though; I asked myself, why did I postpone reading the book? Why did I refuse to finish it the first time I ever opened its pages? As I continued reading, I realized that many of the things happening in my life at that time were created by my inability to clearly state my desires and then take appropriate action; instead, I would focus on how to obtain it. It was very difficult to accept that the not-so-positive things that were happening to me were only the result of my own ineptitude to take action.

To Fail or To Succeed: It's Your Choice is a book that helps us to open our eyes and take responsibility. It helps us to put away our excuses and take action in every aspect of our lives. Page by page, it reveals the importance of our connection to God and reminds us that God is in every one of us. It is a revelation; what happens to us in life is the product of our incapacity to learn how to be. I discovered that we spend our lives focused on having, doing, and the process of things, rather than getting better at just Being on a daily basis.

When I finished reading the book, I felt a new kind of energy; a desire to change my habits and put into practice some of its suggested exercises. Not necessarily the techniques that are mentioned in the context, but beyond them, like the message to better myself, always thinking about the greater good.

I encountered several sections of the book which brought me a great deal of anxiety because the message was directly opposed to the truth I held in my heart about our connection to God, to people and to my own self. However, I can honestly and without a doubt say that the message I got was exactly what I needed then in order to move forward with my life.

Sometimes we do not understand why things happen when they happen to us, and with this book, I understood that everything happens at the right place and time.

I will forever thank my father for giving me the opportunity to write this prologue and reveal my experiences through its reading.

I invite you, the one holding this book in your hands, to enjoy a work that was written to help you improve your life, changing excuses for actions, contingencies for habits, and wanting to be for Being now.

God bless you,

Andrea Hernandez
M.S. in Mathematics and Teaching
New York University
PhD in Mathematics Education
Columbia University

NIGHT AND DAY

An angel of wisdom and an angel of love were in trouble:
The first one kept manifesting ignorance, and the second one much heartache.
How did they manage to realize the situation given that they were in heaven? Because there was no coherence between what the angel of wisdom knew, and the results he got; and in the dark of the night, the deep loneliness made the angel of love shudder.

They both took advantage of their knowledge in order to move indiscriminately between the light and the shadow.

In the shadow, the law of the day is that you suffer, you pay for what you do, and learning is a painful thing to do; while in the light there is grace, all is magic, and miracles are the order of the day.

How curious, why are there creatures that, while living in the light, decide to come down and suffer in the law? What these angels experienced led them to recognize their own wisdom, by focusing on the results and expressing themselves through their hearts.

How did this happen? One day, as they were wandering around in the darkness driven by curiosity, the heavy weight of the emotional shackles caught their wings and they were unable to fly; each one blamed the other, and allowed the worse of their hate and ignorance to come out. They hurt one another so much that pain took over their souls.

They did not want to see each other ever again, and in the midst of such despair, eyes filled with tears and experiencing a pain so deep within their wombs, they begged to God to give them back their light; their plead was so honest that from the heavens came the order to release them immediately.

Without the attachments from the darkness and in the freedom of grace, they recovered their wings and flew away. Now their tears were not of pain, but happiness; their hearts burnt with a love so pure that no human could have imagined, a love beyond emotions and a wisdom that illuminates the world with its example.

They flew freely into eternity, knowing that if they wished to, they could count on one another and the magic of grace. Besides, eternity would unite them, repeatedly, in the light of God.

INTRODUCTION

Is excellence a road or a destination?

Before the birth of the concepts of total quality management and zero error, developed by the Japanese and in vogue during the 70's, it was believed that being successful in life was a thing of destiny.

How far from reality! Today, the most valuable lesson to be extracted from the kaizen theory is that everything is susceptible not only to be achieved but also improved. This theory invites us to identify the best, imitate the best, be equal to the best and become better than the best, keeping in mind there is a difference between imitating someone good and imitating the best. Now, who to imitate and what to imitate? In order to imitate successful people it is of utmost importance to recognize the two most common mistakes: imitating the wrong person, or imitating the wrong strategy from the right person.

When you wish to embark upon the journey of excellence, you must forge the character to imitate only the people or businesses that got the results we are looking for, and used the right strategy.

Nobody can deny the beauty of Luciano Pavarotti's voice, and the way his singing has brought much happiness to thousands of people around the world; however, you would probably choose not to imitate the way he eats, for you would end up with a body like his and could never sing like him. Equally, nobody can deny the importance of Albert Einstein's theory of relativity, which changed the way people thought in the twentieth century. To think that in order to be as genius as Einstein you need to have a love life such as his, would probably result in making your couple very unhappy.

The era of great speakers is behind; now is the time for the doers, the ones who set an example to follow. As such, to lead by example is not the most important thing about leadership... it is the only important thing. However, there are certain strategies that, in the appropriate context, can be of great benefit to us.

Some people could teach us about loyalty, creativity, perseverance, and how to think big; if they would have developed their qualities in a different context and with different goals, they would probably be marketing geniuses and not the creators of such dreadful results for themselves and for humanity; among them, I can think of drug dealers, robbers, assassins, etc.

If we take a judging look at the motto, "There is always a better and easier way of doing things," one may perceive that as we apply this great principle of human creativity we move further along the road of excellence. On the other hand, as soon as someone considers to have found perfection, at that very same moment is manifesting mediocrity and obsoleteness. The 'finished product' syndrome has driven many great executives out of the market, ones who in their moment were thought to be sacred to their organizations.

Just listening to some people talk is enough to know if they belong to the age of continuous improvement; in general, these people focus on the future and speak about successful results. Nevertheless, those whose conversations and dialogues are focused on the past and the obstacles manifest a tendency to failure. Earl Wilson says, "If you did it yesterday and it still seems like a big thing today, then you have not done enough today."

To Fail or To Succeed: It's Your Choice brings our focus to the improvement of the seven most important aspects of any human being: the spiritual, physical, relationship, educational, work, financial and recreational.

It is important to understand that any person, if he so desires, can obtain the same results as others, or he may choose to create new ones. What is remarkable is the fact that in order to succeed or fail in life there is a formula, and we have been applying it unconsciously in the majority of the cases. The purpose of this book is to take the reader by the hand, so that, based on knowledge, he may consciously choose the road he wishes to understand, eliminating from his beliefs such false paradigms as: we are the victims of destiny; what happened was nothing but God's whim, etc., and many other false premises whose sole objective is to hide the fact that we are responsible for a great truth: we are the creators of our own destiny and the universe supports us unconditionally in whatever we choose to believe and create.

PART ONE

"The true leader is willing to conquer himself; his only purpose is to fulfill the mission for which he has been created, to live in the light and surrender to the divine will."

When is too late to love

THE BEGINNING

The dream filled me with questions, and following that divine impulse, hunch or karmic duty, I promised myself I would divulge everything that I experienced on that day through the writing of the book "When is too late to love." However, I did not know I was getting myself ready to become immersed in multiple self-evaluation sessions, and subjected to the most unforgiving source of judgment one can ever encounter: one's own.

I had written the book - a milestone in my life - several years prior; however, the more I read it, the more I was convinced that it did not come from me, but was written through me. Nonetheless, my mind filled up with many questions: if the genius minds of publicity never approved of it, why such title? They considered it deceiving, as if the readers would think of it as a romance novel rather than the manual of excellence it was intended to be.

Most of the people who wrote to me after reading the book had either just come out of a relationship, suffered from some type of terminal illness or had lost a loved one. I never thought the title would captivate them to such a degree, and that it would afford a great measure of peace to their souls and hope for a better tomorrow.

But, what about me? What was happening to me? Although my life kept slowly, yet continuously getting better, the changes did not happen at the speed I would have liked them to. Considering I had more information than the average people in the market, I should have been able to accomplish my goals faster and easier; not forgetting that what is important is not what we accomplish, but the person we become as a result of conquering our dreams. I concluded that precisely because I had written that book – which kept selling more and more – it was important for me to accelerate my own learning process. I promised myself that I would only write something new when I really considered that I had turned into the person I felt I should be.

Nevertheless, I allowed myself to be once more guided by my inner voice, the one that speaks to us so often but we seldom listen to. This time, it ardently invited me to take the pen and fulfill my mission: to write this message, which according to my feelings would help improve the lives of many.

Although I refused to write something new until I had become a master, I was overcome by the urgent need to write To Fail or To Succeed: It's Your Choice.

I remembered something I read in the book *Illusions* by Richard Bach: "We teach best what we most need to learn," and I chose to put on paper the teachings of my master teacher, Mr. Deeb.

The encounter with the Master Teacher

"The synchronicity of life allows you to understand that everything is perfect; each event you attract into your life, as well as each person who comes your way, has a specific message, a lesson, and a specific purpose in your life's plan."

When is too late to love

I can surely say that I met him by chance; However, I know he would be quick to correct me and say that nothing happens by chance and everything makes perfect sense in our lives, and because of that, I would much rather say that it was a coincidence.

The owner of the house I lived in at the time told me she had met a very special being, a man of advanced age that could tell whether one was ready to receive his teachings by just looking at one's hands. His workshops, which were practically free, had changed the meaning of life for thousands of people, making a positive impact on their happiness and wellbeing.

So, what was my life at the time? I was recently divorced and renting a room in a boardinghouse; made just enough money to survive, yet my expenses were greater than my income; I did not have a permanent job, but in order to survive I worked all day in whatever I could find. I went to college at night in order to study something that was not fulfilling. My only thought was to graduate so I could be done with it, hoping that as a professional I would be able to find a better job, one that would pay more money even if I did not like what I would have to do on a daily basis.

I felt life was unfair, and that some people were born with luck while others sucked from the moment they were born. I thought that to be rich or poor, happy or unhappy, was a matter of destiny. I had very low self-image and self-esteem. I thought there were some people gifted by God, happy beings filled with prosperity in every single way, while others, for reasons I could not understand, were born to face uncountable tests and obstacles in life.

I was sure the planet was ruled by injustice, and worse of all, I could not find much sense in life; every day was just as the day before; everything was a repetition, and my discontented heart made the day-to-dayness fill my every day with nostalgia. Happiness was out of my reach, and it only manifested itself during short, evasive moments; at some party, some meeting with friends, or some random activity that drove monotony briefly out of my life. My relationship with God was pretty much distant, and the way I rebelled against life spoke of me as an adolescent lost in the desert of his own ignorance. In that context, the possibility of meeting someone that could change the route and the road I was taking in life seemed very exciting and it made me very happy. It did not take me long to make an appointment with him. Two days later, I was sitting in an office face to face with the person that would have the greatest impact in my life: Mr. Richard Deeb.

While sitting in the waiting room, my heart pounded with an unusual force and some uncontrollable thought haunted my mind: What if this man told me that I was not ready to receive his teachings yet? About twenty minutes later – this seemed like an eternity to me – his assistant, Flor Mary, informed me that Mr. Deeb invited me to come into his office.

When I saw him I was impressed, I knew I was in front of someone special. His sole presence commanded respect and wisdom. His smile illuminated a face that denoted old wisdom – I figured he was about seventy years old – and brought happiness to his surroundings. He was tall, erect and slim, with a deep look in his eyes that could see past appearances and read between the lines, connecting with the sacred and perfect part of whoever came to him, at the very moment he said 'hello.' In order to recover from the impact of his presence, I immediately asked him, "How are you doing Mr. Deeb?" Without hesitation and looking me straight in the eyes, he answered: "Marvelously my son, marvelously"

At once, he took my hand, gave it a careful look and smiled, knowing the synchronicity of life had predetermined that moment, and that I was the one he had been waiting for.

He talked about my qualities and defects; it seemed as if he had known me my whole life, and pointed out several things I must learn in this life. He seemed obviously pleased when he announced that I was accepted to take his courses. He authorized me to enroll immediately – most of the people had to wait anywhere from two to three months in order to get a spot – and assured me we would see each other again, and that he would be delighted to share more of the information with me. He made it clear that our next reunion would be at the end of the course, which many called metaphysics and others, self-knowledge; he preferred to simply call it "Mr. Deeb's course."

Although our interview was very short, I sensed I had had a meeting with destiny and I was getting ready to discover the purpose of my life at a more conscious level. We bid each other farewell like old friends, and even though I wished to stay, I could not find a proper excuse to do it; he also did not show a sign of wanting to share another second of his time with me. He said good-bye using one of the two phrases I would hear him say the most during our following sessions: "God bless you, my son." The other phrase was, "Marvelously, son, marvelously." I left the premises in a state of awe and ecstasy; I knew I had encountered someone very special, but what I did not know was that because of him my life would begin to change in every single way and for the better.

I pondered about every second of that meeting and I enrolled in his courses. Once I completed that cycle, I made a new appointment with Mr. Deeb. I could not help but wonder why no one knew of his teachings, and the most astonishing thing of all was to think that, having all of that wisdom, he had never written a book. When I asked him about it, his answered was: "Because in this life I came to learn to be humble, son, and I do not wish to do anything that may feed my ego."

The course lasted seven weeks, with an intensity of two hours a day, from Monday to Friday, and even though Mr. Deeb himself did not teach it, I felt his presence accompanying us at each and every conference. Facilitators chosen by him taught the courses; the first course was taught by a forty some lady. The best times of the day were the hours I spent taking the courses because I really loved the subjects. Every second of those weeks filled my days with much happiness and wisdom.

The end of the seminar was surprisingly unimaginable; we had to so some exercises that allowed us to have a two-way conversation with God. Not only did we pray and give thanks, but we also learned to ask him questions, listen to him and obtain conscious answers from God.

I was so fulfilled by what I learned at the seminars that I took them all over again, but with different instructors; It caught my attention the fact that even though it was the same subject, it was always presented in a way pertinent to the audience. I felt as if I had gone to a brand new seminar, completely different, which led me to repeat it several times more, and every time I had the same experience.

About Mr. Deeb's teachings

There are two types of people in the world. Those who are victims of destiny, are asleep, things happen to them and are used to leaving things for later, their lives repeat monotonously over and over again. The second type is those who make things happen; they know they only have twenty-four hours, so they fill their days with many events and experiences. These people are used to sleeping tired and live every day as if it was the last day of their lives, making themselves one hundred percent responsible for their results, knowing where they are in life is the outcome of what they have or have not done, and their lives are filled with continuous and exciting new days.

Success is the progressive realization of a dream; it is a road yet to be enjoyed, not a destiny to arrive at. 'Do not be hasty,' used to say Mr. Deeb to me, 'There is nowhere to go. Live this moment to the fullest because it is the only thing you really have. Discover the dreams that lay in your heart and focus on making them come true; this will make your life abundant and you will be able to enter the road of success.'

He asked me to memorize the ten characteristics of a person that follows a model of excellence:

1. They focus on solutions, not on problems.

2. They know everything can be improved.

3. They recognize themselves as unlimited beings, limited only by their own ignorance.

4. They dream big, have clear goals and a coherent action plan to achieve their dreams.

5. They have a high regard for their own self and an adequate sense of self-image. They believe in God, in themselves, in people and what they do.

6. Their thoughts focus permanently on their goals, as if they already accomplished them, and they carefully select the kind of information they feed themselves through the five senses.

7. They are natural born visionaries; able to see the glass half full when others see it half-empty. They can see a paradise where others see a mere piece of land.

8. They are quick to admit when they make a mistake, making the most of the experience and performing the necessary actions to prevent it from happening again.

9. When they speak about a commitment, they know a human being should not commit to anything ninety nine percent (just did what they could); there is only one kind of commitment and that is one hundred percent (he did what was necessary). A TOTAL commitment occurs when the person does what is necessary, and everyone knows they did what was necessary when they obtain the results they were looking for.

10. They know how to eliminate all excuses from their hearts, and recognize that only a mediocre person hides behind an excuse; to be a little mediocre, give a little excuse, and to be a bigger mediocre give a bigger one.

Hoping to leave me with something to ponder about, he gave me some lessons learned a few years prior at the school of leadership, for he knew that once he gave them to me they would put me on the road of excellence.

❖ To arrive early is to be on time; to be on time is to arrive late and to arrive late is to disrespect everyone.

❖ The communicator is responsible for the communication. As such, it is irresponsible to say that someone misunderstood us, it is best to say: I have not made myself clear.

❖ It is important to recognize there is no better time to enter the road of excellence than the present moment, not any other; and the ideal place is right here, not anywhere else.

❖ If not you, then who else? If not now, then when? In addition, if it is not what you are doing right now, then what else do you have to do?

He also gave me Confucius' premises for success: "If you wish to succeed you need three things: Relate to people correctly, be competent in what you do, and know yourself."

Most impactful lessons from the seminars I took with Mr. Deeb's appointed instructors

The most impactful subject at the beginning of the seminar was the concept of God and our connection to Him through our vibration. God's general qualities were defined as omnipresent, omnipotent, omnisapient and eternal.

Omnipresent: God is everywhere; then, it is impossible for anything or anyone to become separate from God. Whatever you do, wherever you are, you will always live in the heart of God. They invited us to feel the Divine Presence on a daily basis, with every breath, in whatever we see and touch, and to be capable of seeing God in every person that crosses our way. They taught us the cause of many of our greatest evils was the idea of being mentally separate from God, and this idea was something we have been taught throughout the ages; it makes us feel unworthy of God and of the many blessings inherent to each and every one of us. They said if we refused to live under the rule of this false idea of separation, the majority of our problems would disappear. They continually reminded us to say these two phrases:

"God with me, who against me"
"I am capable of all in God who brings me strength"

Omniscient: God knows it all, and when we live in the heart of God, all information, creativity, wisdom, enlightenment and knowledge is in us as well; because of this, in order to connect to higher levels of knowledge I just needed to raise my own vibration and learn to obtain answers from within me. Up until there the information was acceptable; our self-esteem and self-image kept improving, especially when we remembered God made us in his image. However, to develop the ability to apply this information to the beggar in the street, a killer or a robber, or simply to the one whose lifestyle we despised, that, in and of itself, was the major leagues, something worthy of the enlightened ones. In those times, I remember, it was very hard to quit making false gods and mustering the will to listen to our own inner wisdom, to believe more in ourselves.

Omnipotent: God can do anything; after a simple analysis, we concluded this divine quality made miracle workers out of all of us, and the more we feel our union with God, the greater our ability to break our limitations and perform miracles. No wonder it has been determined those people who have succeeded in life have lived in communion with God. People of all religions succeed, therefore, it is not required to belong to a specific religion nor is there one true religion; the coherence between the capacity of the individual to follow the rules of their religion while keeping a close relationship with God, is enough for that person to manifest his unlimited capacities. It was transcendental to learn to feel worthy of God, and to create a relationship so tight that when we communicated with Him we would encounter the most loyal of friends, who accepts us as we are and does not judge or criticize us, for we were made in his own image.

Eternal: God has no beginning and no end. We discovered that even we, who live in the heart of God, are eternal and our existence transcends beyond time and space. To heal our relationship with god – they explained – is the easiest way to improve all aspects of our lives; it makes us worthy of all blessings because we recognize they have already been given to us.

They repeatedly said that not one soul could get lost because nothing is outside of God, and that heaven and hell are human creations that point to the large gap between our precarious way of being and our innate excellence: the former represents our limitations, poverty, sickness, ignorance, suffering, resentment and the need to make others suffer in order to gain something when we live in the shadow; the second one represents what we really are: unlimited, light, prosperity, wisdom, health, happiness, love and many other holy things.

In this road to self-discovery, we were waking up to and walking from our inner hell toward our inner heaven, and from our wicked way of seeing and behaving in life until we turned into a divine expression, a perfect manifestation of God, always living for the greater good and the highest of outcomes.

About vibration

They informed us that every element in the cosmos vibrates, and that vibration allows us to connect to a higher or lower level of consciousness, light, happiness, richness and health. In other words, we are magnets that attract into our lives what resonates with our level of vibration. Therefore, it is truly foolish to expect prosperity if one is vibrating with the frequency of poverty; to expect health if we vibrate with the frequency of sickness; to expect to live in the light when we vibrate with the frequency of darkness.

Because of this, all wishes that are not accompanied by the corresponding level of vibration are mere fantasies, while all wishes accompanied by the appropriate level of vibration turn to cosmic orders that will materialize at the right moment. To take care of our vibration is to take care of our expected results; thus, in order to better our results one must improve one's level of vibration so that one can connect with that innate capacity to attract greater results into our existence. They also taught that life is like a tall building and our vibration is the elevator that takes us from one floor to another; what we find in each floor cannot be changed, but what we can do is choose our own destiny by increasing our vibration in order to go to the appropriate floor, the one that holds all the things we want.

Every being vibrates with poverty or richness, sickness or health, sadness or happiness, light or darkness, resentment or forgiveness, hate or love, loneliness or companionship, etc.

Now, the question is, where does our level of vibration come from? We were taught it is the result of five things: *our thoughts, feelings, words, actions, and our spiritual, mental and physical diet.*

Hateful thoughts generate a vibration of hate; thoughts of security and forgiveness generate a vibration of security and forgiveness; thoughts of poverty generate a vibration of poverty; thoughts of abundance generate a vibration of abundance. The same thing happens with our words, actions and feelings. We understood that when we properly choose what we eat, we properly choose our vibration.

About the contacts

When we finished Mr. Deeb's course, we had to practice a meditation that we called 'contacts,' and it allowed us to listen consciously to God.

On the first day, we wrote whatever thoughts came to our mind, kind of like trying to make our subconscious less busy; on the second day - the second contact - we asked specific questions and obtained specific answers according to our needs, which filled us with much satisfaction. This was our graduation in order to enter the road of the light warrior, the true road to self-discovery. It filled us with a sense of indescribable power, one that undeniably erased from our intellect any doubts we could have had about the existence of God. From that moment on, each participant began to experience a more practical approach to spirituality, a greater level of awareness of existence and security in themselves, as well as the future.

When we asked Mr. Deebs about the accuracy of our contacts, he usually said to us that, beyond words, the important thing was to verify that the words we wrote made sense to us and that its application improved the quality of our lives. Anyhow – he insisted, – every human being, whether he recognizes it or not, knows exactly when he is on the right path and whether information is coming from the right source.

The happiness we felt on the days we had contacts turned those nights into holy nights, announcing God's re-birth within our hearts. I do not fear I am wrong when I say the happiness we felt was equal to or greater than the happiness experienced on Christmas Eve, which is a lot to say when one thinks about it, for Christmas Eve is the most magical night of the year.

He also said that sometimes all we write is our mental creations, fruit of our intellect and its ability to control our thoughts. Because of this, instead of contacting the Divine within our being, we communicate with our subconscious. The mastery to learn to differentiate between one and the other would come gradually as a consequence of practicing these meditations. He insisted on the importance of practicing continuous discernment: discernment can never be surrendered because it is what guards us from the valley of illusions and unfounded fantasies.

Having clarified that entire subject, Mr. Deeb allowed me to write down one of the contacts I experienced toward the end of the course, for it is one that continues to amaze me to this day. I believe without a doubt that it was God who spoke to me; however, I leave it to your own judgment, to choose whether it came from God or my ego.

Contact with God and his message on how we come to this planet and what makes a difference in our results

Every human being has a guardian angel, but the guardian angel chooses us. Who could it be from among us? Is the question that riddles you hearts?

Angels are beings of light and their essence is known to be unlimited. They live in a world where everything is possible; there are no limits. Their hearts radiate love, meaning, acceptance, understanding, comprehension, admiration and an unmistakable desire to serve. Their faces show true wisdom, a wisdom that guides the evolution of minerals, vegetables, animals, humans or any other form they choose. They can move from the celestial realm to the human, according to their intentions.

Where they live, there is no place for the intellectual mind, everything is felt and communication is heart to heart; differences in form are accepted, no one envies any one, they recognize each other as inseparable, unique beings. The harmony brought about by their unity makes them invincible. They take delight in the never-ending game of understanding the differences created by humans. The perfect analogy is that of the jewel maker, capable of turning the same piece of gold into an infinite number of forms, and no matter how hard he insists on changing the karats and the form, the essence of the jewel could never changed.

The greatest difference is undoubtedly the fact they are perfectly and completely aware of their essence, while on Earth, men and women are victims of their own ignorance because they think they are the reflection of their appearance. The confusion between what is real and what is not creates a lot of suffering among the inhabitants of Earth. That pain turns into a path to self-discovery, and only when the individual becomes enlightened, when he discovers that he is inseparable from God and takes responsibility for his conscious or unconscious creations that is when he really gets to experience acceptance, then, his limitations disappear along with the unhappiness they created. Now, in order to honor the veracity of this tale, we must understand that every atom that composes the All - the great God, the Universe, Ether, Energy or whatever name you wish to give - is made out of love, justice and wisdom.

The greatest of them all is the one who does not allow himself to be trapped by form and is capable of seeing the greatness in every being; is capable of going from the skin to the heart of matters. It almost seems profane, but the guardian angel would have to teach the one he guides to see God in everything; in the water, the animal, the plant and every human being whether it is black, white, Indian, Jewish or Christian; in the preacher, in those who serve, and even the ones who rob, kill... in other words, he is capable of seeing God in the air he breathes, in EVERYTHING.

For this select team of light beings it is very clear what the root of all the suffering on Earth is. These are beings whose forms are mere fun, conscious creations; for them, *to serve* is a synonym for *Being*, and as such, to be selected or chosen is a reward, so the form does not matter; any form is alright.

What is the mission of these beings? To take on the role of guardian angels; to accompany human beings during their lifetime; to help them overcome their obstacles so that when they discover their potentials they can go from the shadow to the light. Besides, their mission is to sensitize men and fill them with compassion toward their fellow brothers and sisters, this way, they will understand that limits are self-imposed and most important, that the source of everything created and the place where miracles are born is in the heart of every human being.

The choice is very simple: those who are present come filled with much enthusiasm, yet in a complete state of detachment, which confirms they are beings of light. They exist to fulfill the Divine will. They would never question it or think it could be otherwise. They are known for their deep sense of devotion and obedience; well acquainted with the concept of the purpose of life and our synchronicity with the Universe. In their hearts, no one is ahead of anyone; and if not in that moment, maybe a second later, a year, or even an eternity later. What really matters is their willingness to serve when someone needs them.

You could hear many people clapping, some saying their 'good byes', others shouting 'good luck,' and in the chosen angel's face, a look of utter humility and gratefulness. These meetings ended with an invocation to the light, sacred chants, and a ceremony of indescribable love.

About our capacity

On this planet called Earth, God chose to create the human being, and when he did, he made him in his own image; He created man and woman without limitations, wise and powerful. As time went by, many men forgot their true essence and a new race of beings was born; a race that, ignorant of their true origin, took delight in their precarious ways and chose to fill themselves with limitations, justifying their results as the only logical outcome of their ignorance. Their differences were so absurdly contradicting that some had the guts to think God's sense of humor and injustice were unforgiving. The truth was that God had created us - with no exception - as unlimited beings of light that had the freewill to choose.

From the beginning, human beings were created to manifest the glory of God and they possessed divine powers. Unfortunately, because so many would not understand the extent of their own capacities, they could not realize that we all have the same capacity; that in essence, there is no difference between the saint and the thief, the ignorant and the well-studied, the young and the old, the rich and the poor, the healthy and the sick.

How could human beings discover and apply their powers to the pursuit of their dreams? Mainly, they would have to discover, recognize and identify these powers. They would also need to understand the ultimate secret about our limitations: that the more that you accept you can become separate from God, the more limitations you will have; and the more that you accept it is impossible to become separate from God, the less limitations that you have and you become capable of performing miracles.

About the powers we possess to create quality of life

- The power of our connection to the Divine.
- The power of your connection to yourself and your dreams.
- The power of our connection to the environment and others.
- The power of the master mind.
- The power of the frequency of vibration.
- The power to believe and create.
- The power of action.
- The power of feelings.
- The power of association.
- The power of determination.

- The power of focus.
- The power of attraction.
- The power of projection.
- The power of choice.
- The power of physical, mental and spiritual nourishment.
- The power of prayer.
- The power of spiritual practices.
- The power of meditation.
- The power of contemplation.
- The power of faith.
- The power of love.

Each being receives these mentioned powers as an imprint at birth, and they remain as a record in their hearts; it is there where they must search repeatedly if they wish to remember them.

All human beings have the same capacity, and once they discover it they will have freed themselves from the bothersome feeling that they are "victims of destiny." They will take responsibility for their creations right in the moment, empowering themselves and taking delight in the art of living, of living life learning, growing and moving forward with the art of being aware of their creations. The hard disc of that human computer, which is called 'the brain,' will remain the same; there will be no differences on the planet and the capacity of the saint will be the same as that of the thief.

What will be the greatest difference? The programs, which will be slowly and gradually installed in the cells of every human being from the moment of conception, and in the human brain from the moment of birth.

Whatever information you receive through your senses – whether you listen to it asleep or awake, whatever you watch, smell, touch or taste – is recorded forever, and it will condition your destiny whether you know it or not. Hopefully, sooner than later you will take responsibility for what you take in through your five senses, whether consciously or unconsciously, because that is the food for your thoughts: nothing can leave your mind that has not first entered it. The mental programs set the difference: whatever you record there, no matter how logical or not it seems, will be true. You never stop recording, and whatever predominant thought you have in your mind will soon materialize.

SECOND PART

"For you, everything is possible, even becoming what you are not yet."

When is too late to love

THE REUNION

Although several months had passed, it was amazing for me to see how little I missed him and how much he had stayed with me during that period; even though I never saw him while I was taking the seminars, it was as if he was always there with me.

When I saw him again, I had a weird sensation, as if we knew each other from way before or even as if he had always been the master teacher and I had been the disciple. Our greeting was so simple and authentic that my soul appeared to have memories from other lives, I had the sensation I had already lived that moment. He asked me:

– "What did you like about the seminar you just finished?" and without a pause continued, "What questions do you have?"

His questions brought the part of me that narrates my internal stories back to reality, for it hallucinated imagining so many things.

– "I was fascinated by the understanding that what I have always looked for is inside of me, and that God is not a foreign entity that I must look for in some place outside of me, rather that my body is his temple and my heart is his home. It has given me two things: what I needed to be more secure about myself, and an absolute desire to conquer my dreams. Oh! Yes! And I also feel happy to know that no matter where I am or what I do, it is impossible to become separate from Him!" I answered.

– "Your understanding and acceptance of something of such significance, and your enthusiasm to begin living a different kind of life fills me with much happiness." He replied.

– "However, the seminar did make me ask some questions of which I am not certain." I added.

– "That is great news," he said. "It means you are processing the information that you received. Ask all the questions you need, I am here to answer them."

– "Well, I did not quite understand the whole thing about the guardian angel." I said.

– "Every one of us has a guardian angel that cares for, protects and orients us." He answered. "For the first seven years of our lives, they are allowed to guide and take care of us even if we have not asked them to. After those seven years, we need to invoke them on a daily basis in order to have their protection, but many spend their whole lives without ever communicating with their guardian angel and without knowing or using this wisdom; they waste such a precious source of unlimited power. The greatest counselor, guide, who can take us through the road to self-realization, is the same one who usually spends our whole lives waiting for us to summon his presence. Even though his job is to help, he cannot intervene and must respect the universal law of freewill. Therefore, guardian angels only come to the aid of those who ask for their help."

– "Alright then." I said. "Now my second question is this: If we are totally unlimited beings, how come some fail and others succeed in life?"

– "Some fail and others succeed, consciously or unconsciously, some follow the road to success and others the road to failure; both roads are very similar to one another. Therefore, if one does not apply the appropriate principles, one can get confused very easily. This is an excellent opportunity to give you a gift, taking advantage of this sunny afternoon. Today, some choose to sleep the heat away while others work more diligently because they feel invigorated. You will start receiving the information that will make your dreams come true; I will show you **the road of success** step-by-step, and you will understand that To Fail or To Succeed: It's Your Choice. In order to learn this, we will invest several weeks of our time, but these days will turn into a very fruitful time of your life. You will receive information that you will digest when the time is right, until such moment when the information will have turned to inner wisdom."

–"What?!" I said in awe. "There is a road of success!"

– "Yes," Replied Mr. Deeb. "To fail or to succeed in life is your choice; it is not a matter of destiny or a random event. A successful person achieves what he sets out to accomplish; a looser says he is going to do something and does not accomplish it. If you say 'I am going to practice this sport,' you will be successful if you do, whether you win or lose in the game; however, if you set out to win the sport, you will only be successful when you triumph. Let us commence your lessons on the road of success."

THE ROAD OF SUCCESS
The Formula

First, let us take a look at the formula and then we will analyze it with more details: The results obtained by human beings are the product of their beliefs plus their habits. As such, those who know exactly what they want, and get it, obtain successful results. On the other hand, people who hesitate about what they desire will often get the results they do not want.

– "This diagram has a very detailed explanation of the road of success." He said. "Analyze it, and as soon as you are ready, let me know what you consider is the most important part of it."

—"Thank you." I said, though I was perplexed. I did not analyze anything at all; I could only see one route, a map that any child could easily understand. It was very elemental. Then, why is it so hard to be successful in life? The only answer I could come up with was *ignorance*. Minutes later, I broke my silence, and said, "The most important thing is to determine the result we want, to know exactly what we want." I said, filled with pride like a little boy who knows he just gave the right answer and is expecting to be rewarded.

— "Perfect," He replied, "you are on your way. People's lives and circumstances would be much different if everybody would just ask themselves one question before doing anything new, and that question is: What do I wish to obtain as a result of doing this? In addition, if their wish is to solve a problem, they could lay out the result they want ahead of time. For one, they would probably feel highly motivated by the time they begin to do whatever it is they want to do; on the other hand, the answer to their problem would certainly be the right one, and it would bring them a greater level of wisdom than they could have thought of. Now, let us begin the analysis of this wonderful road of success. I reiterate the fact that we are going step-by-step, but be very careful because the simplicity of it may be a source of disillusionment for your intellect, which is used to doing things the hard and complicated way. Very often, we forget that the simplest and most elemental of things hold the wisest answers to our problems. In order to go beyond your intellect and listen to the wisest part of you – which speaks to you via your senses, - I recommend that you take a deep breath and focus on seeing the road of success, step-by-step. You will understand that to fail or succeed is a choice, although many think to the contrary, mainly those irresponsible ones who blame destiny for what they get in life. Let us begin with the most elemental form of the formula:

Beliefs + Habits = Results

All human beings' actions generate a result, and this is true for all areas of our lives. It is only when you specifically ask yourself, *what do I want?* That you become capable of evaluating whether the reality of your world reflects the results you desire. We should ask ourselves this wise and simple question more often. So, now the formula takes on a new component:

Beliefs + Habits = Successful results

Now, where do beliefs come from and how do they lead to the establishment of your habits, in other words, your second nature or wisdom? It is important to know and remember that wisdom is not about the information that you possess, but rather in your habits, in other words, your frequent, daily actions. Take note of all the variables on the road of success:

THE ROAD OF SUCCESS

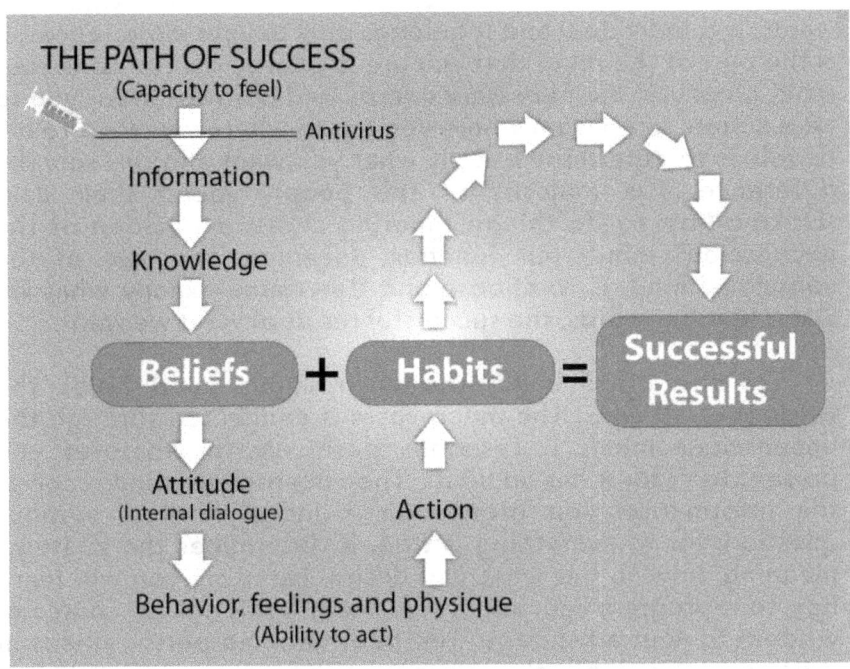

EVERYTHING IS MIND

Learn this universal law: everything is mind, listen well, everything. Of the world of possibilities, you create your reality through your images and words; this is what people call 'thinking.' It is important to know the role of the mind. The mind has always recorded all of your experiences throughout eternity. The mind is made manifest in every atom of the universe; at an individual scale it manifests through you, in every cell of your being; and at a language level it manifests through your brain.

The mind is divided in conscious and unconscious

The conscious mind is designed to determine what one wants; it is individual and it belongs only to your experiences; it is the part of the mind that you are in charge of. The conscious mind gives you the necessary energy and motivation for you to take action, to go from where you are to where you want to be. Its role is to determine exactly what you want and this sets the difference. The majority of the people spend their days thinking how to do things, ignoring this is a function of the unconscious mind; our function, meaning, the role of the conscious mind, is to choose and determine exactly what we want, in other words, the successful result of what we want.

On the other hand, the unconscious mind holds the wisdom of all ages. The macrocosm is connected through the unconscious mind; it responds positively to whatever you present to it, for it has no limits. The unconscious mind receives the information you present in a literal fashion, without question; for it, everything is true. It determines the strategy, meaning, how to get what you desire. Later on, you will learn how to reprogram yourself in order to use this eternal source of wisdom to your advantage. The information a person needs in order to achieve his objectives is in the unconscious mind; it knows what is best for every person, and there is not one unconscious mind that knows better than other does because in reality they are all one and the same, one mind. The unconscious mind is in charge of developing the strategies; as soon as you desire something it knows exactly how to make your wish come true, the 'how' is the unconscious mind's business. In order to materialize it, you need to learn certain principles, which I will explain as we continue to review the road of success. For now, keep in mind that as you focus on the 'how,' the tendency will be to feel tired because you are going out of the scope of your capacities. In general, when someone feels unmotivated is because his or her focus is in the 'how.'

When you are motivated or encounter people who live continually motivated, you can verify their focus is on what they want, on the successful result. For example, when you get up in the morning you consciously choose to go to the bathroom, immediately, the unconscious mind gives the necessary orders so that it can happen. That means, it gives the order to the muscles of the body so that it can move and go to the bathroom. The same thing happens with any kind of order you present it with. To have breakfast or go to work; you decide what you want and the unconscious mind takes care of the 'how.' Ninety five percent of our decisions are unconscious (how), and only five percent of them are conscious (what). Hence, it is your duty to be precise about what you want and the universe will take care of the details to make your dreams come true.

Here, we encounter the first reason why some people are successful and others not. The first ones spend their time determining exactly what they want; to know how it looks, smells, tastes, feels and sounds, as well as when they want it, where, with who and why they want it. The second ones almost never get what they want; they constantly focus on how to obtain things, many times without first taking the time to clearly determining the successful result of what they want. The 'how' can never motivate an individual, only the 'what.' This is the reason so many people end up paralyzed by the analysis process, because they want to know how to do things; their mind paralyzes them until they choose to go the right way. Many of these people suffer from depression mostly due to over thinking, rather than acting; many times, the depression will go away as soon as there is any kind of movement.

The first step is to determine the successful result. It is of utmost importance to remember that to think is to create; and in this order of ideas, Descartes said, "I think, therefore I exist;" and you really are creating when you go through the process of determining the successful result of what you desire, without limits, which are the usual result of the collective ignorance. When you are capable of wielding the pen of imagination and color your own dreams, along with every little detail, without care of what people think is possible or impossible, that is when you are thinking; otherwise you are merely reproducing other people's thoughts. The greatest thinkers in history are those capable of imagining the future down to the smallest of details, and begin to build it in the present.

We are built to choose and determine what we want, from material things all the way to our purpose in life. If you wish to live motivated, be conscious of the successful result of what you do. On the other hand, if you wish to motivate others get used to talking to them about the successful result of what they are doing. If you, or anybody else you know, do not act, do not try to put pressure on you or him, just take some time to evaluate your motives for they may not be that inspiring anymore.

– "Let us slow down here please," I said, "what is this inspiration thing about?"

– "In order to act, you need to have an objective that inspires you into action. If you wish for someone to take action, focus your energy on making the successful result very clear for this person. To know exactly what you want is to have the greatest part of your dream already materialized. If you learn to determine what motivates you and others into action, you will have the world at your feet. Yes, the motives are practically the same as the results you wish to obtain, the successful results. You must not assume anything, it is better to ask frequently and you will know it exactly, because whatever you think motivates someone can be very different from what in fact motivates him. Teach people to use their imagination, to draw their dreams in their mind as if they already got it and you will be a great source of inspiration in their lives; you will fill their hearts and instigate power into their present being.

– "In all honesty, I think it is quite manipulative to use what I know in order to get people to act or do something." I replied.

– "Manipulation happens when you secretly desire - you disguise your motives - and make your personal objective look like it is theirs. What I am teaching you is something rather different: in one hand, that you need to have a clear image of your personal motives and the successful result you desire; on the other hand, to help others clarify their own personal motives and successful results, and by doing so you assist them in their personal journey through the application of principles of success."

– "Many times I have known what I want." I added, "However, I have not been able to accomplish all my dreams. In fact, what I really desire with all my heart, I have yet to obtain. What do you think is the reason?"

– "That is not entirely true." Said Mr. Deebs. "Maybe you have a general idea of what you want, but not an idea of exactly what you want, with precision. For example, people wish to travel, have a house of their own, a new car, study, go shopping, go to nice restaurants, help other people and sustain an excellent state of health. Is that knowing exactly what you want?"

– "Of course not!" I said, feeling quite proud of my answer. At least I thought so at first, but unfortunately, as I further analyzed what he had just said, I found the correct answer. "They need to know, for example, where they want to travel to, when, if by plane, with what airline, with whom, for how long...in short, they need to give as many details as possible to the unconscious mind so it can help you materialize your dream faster. If it is a house they want, they need to state how big they want it – how many square feet, - how many rooms, how many floors, how many bathrooms, what style and the interior design details."

– "You have said it!" He said to me. "The more details, the better. If you wish to be successful, the first step is to become a master of details so in the case anybody asks you what you want, you can automatically express your desire without hesitation, without having to think about it, the same way you say your name. It is important to pay close attention to what you feel once you get the result you want. Observe the way you feel, they will never lie to you; they can tell you whether you are happy or something is missing, or maybe what you desire is not actually good for you. You can determine all of that by learning to observe consciously the way you feel about something. It is also true that once you clearly establish what you desire, and in fact you really desire it, the quickest way to materialize it is by feeling, thinking and acting as if it is already been done, as if you already have it. Be certain there is no way in heaven it will not materialize when and how you want it to happen."

– "What should I do in order to be specific about my desire and materialize it?" I asked.

– "There are three very important steps to follow." He continued to explain. "They will help you to achieve your results faster:

1. To know exactly what you want, determining its ecology, always desiring the greatest good for all and for the highest of ends. This is transcendental, otherwise you will be the mockery of a creator, someone for whom the end justifies the means; this kind of thinking is not encouraging, it limits and gives birth to creations that you regret in the future. As soon as you are certain that you have been eco-friendly in your creation, just focus on the details making sure you involve all five senses in the process, determining when, where and who you wish to share your dream with.

2. Frame your expectations correctly. Always remember, you will not get in life what you desire but what you expect to receive. I must stress here this point because most of the times people have very clear, concrete and beautiful dreams, but deep inside they do not expect them to ever come to happen. When expressed as a positive polarity that expectation is what is called faith; the opposite, or its negative polarity, is called fear.

3. Allow things to happen. This is perhaps the most important step; it consists of including the right feelings

which allow for the flow of energy to your advantage; feelings of happiness, patience, certainty, and mainly gratefulness. This might be the reason the master Jesus Christ used to suggest to give thanks even before receiving the blessings we were asking for.

In summary, to know what you want, be confident it will come true and be thankful for it before you even get it; this will accelerate the materialization of your dreams.

– "If I have asked God for something that is not good for me, in which other way can I know this besides being able to feel it?" I asked.

– "God always answers our prayers, and normally has three different types of answers to give to our prayers:

- It will materialize right at the moment that you want it to,
- Or later on because it is more convenient for you to get it in the future,
- Or maybe he has something better in store for you, better than what you are asking for. Just be patient and wait.

The truth is that God always answers our prayers. Right this moment when you are learning the first step on the road of success, it is important to generate or create an anchor to never forget it."

– "An anchor?" I replied.

– "A way to automatically record something." He said. "For example, lifting your thumb is a way to remind your mind that everything is alright. To smile is an anchor that reflects happiness. One of the most recognized anchors, and that is known to be most effective, is to place the palm of your hand on your chest when you are making a promise, or a decree. Place your hand on your chest as much as you can and say the following aloud: I am happy, I am successful; or the affirmation you need in order to address a certain situation. Looking directly at your left eye while standing in front of a mirror and declaring your affirmations is an anchor that connects you directly to your unconscious, generating a kind of self-hypnosis that helps to materialize what you want faster than normal."

– "What would be the anchor for this first step?" I asked Mr. Deeb.

– "Whenever you are doing something, bring the image of Superman into your mind because he is the image of a superhuman being, or a crazy man wearing his underwear over his pants, it depends on how you look at it. If you know exactly why you are performing a certain action, then you are assuming the role of Superman; but if you do not have a clear image of the successful result and you still take action, you are assuming the role of someone who has not realized he is wearing his underwear over his pants. You can do this exercise as much as you want, like when you get up in the morning, determining whether you have a clear picture of the successful result of your day; when you relate to someone, establishing the successful result of the moment you are sharing; when you wish to learn something new; when you want to travel; when you wish to work; always establish what the successful result looks like in the first place. There is no good or bad, only the right motive; to really establish why you are doing something means you are being honest."

– "Wouldn't this mean that we are becoming square minded, calculating and selfishly interested?" I asked. I automatically asked Mr. Deeb every question that came to my mind, without questioning myself in any way.

– "No." He answered. "It is applying the first principle of success, to know exactly what you want. From the day you were born and throughout your life, you will be going from point A, the place where you are, to point B, the place you wish to be; to clearly determine point B is the best way to start on the road. Besides, in our brain we have this organ known as the reticular activating system, in charge of eliminating the information we do not need in order to get to where we want. If we do not correctly establish point B, we will lose a lot of time because we will be inundated with distractions; the reticular activating system keeps us focused. For example, take a couple of minutes to do this exercise: Look around you and see where there is something with the color red, and then, at the count of three, focus on finding something with the color yellow; you will be amazed to find that the first time the reticular activating system made you focus only on whatever had the color red, even though there was a lot of yellow around you.

The same thing happens with our goals; eliminate the distractions that keep you from them. To begin working toward your goals not having a clear end in your mind is a huge mistake. Get used to clearly determining what you want before taking action and you will get on the road of success. When you start something new, your first thought must be to establish exactly what B looks like; even better, the place where you want to be or what you wish to obtain, and the clearer it is, the easier it will be to follow the road to its materialization.

– "Then, what about those who preach about living in the now and stop living in the future, are they wrong?" I asked.

– "No," replied Mr. Deebs, "on the contrary. It is necessary to bring B to the present moment in order to live more fully in point A; faith in the future brings strength to the present. One of the reasons so many people wander this world like zombies is because they have not clearly established what they desire in point B, so they lack motivation in life. Even beings who consider themselves highly spiritual and have given up on the material things of the world have determined their point B in the divine, and they know exactly what that point B is; this allows them to give themselves to meditation or prayer for hours or days at a time. The problem is not that you need to stop enjoying the present, but the evasion of the self by fantasizing a myriad of things all over the place and that make no sense at all, and that in the end take the self away from being in the here and now. Quite the contrary in fact, to bring point B to the present is to create, in a very concrete way, what you wish to obtain tomorrow; it is using our capacity to create in the here and now; it is to recognize our unlimited power to create.

Clearly establish where you are (A) and where you want to be (B) in the following areas of your life; If you do not where you are, you have already arrived:

- **Spiritual**
- **Physical**
- **Relationships**
- **Education**
- **Occupation**
- **Economic**
- **Recreation**

– "So, what about someone who studies a career in university and focuses on being a great student in order to graduate with honors, and hopefully land an excellent job position with the expectations of having a wonderful future?" I asked.

– "If you follow closely, this person would not be correctly applying the first step toward success, because the first thing is to know what it means to be a successful professional of that particular career, what he would like to be in the future, where he would like to work, how much money he would like to make. In short, if he knows the details of how he would like to live his future job position, for sure he will be a better student in the present moment."

– "Is it all about acceptance, dedication to clearly establish point B before taking any action in point A, and being patient?" I wondered.

– "Yes," He responded, "it is very much important to accept, it is the key to happiness. Besides, to clearly establish point B, first principle of success; to be patient – peace and science – is the greatest virtue any mortal being can possess, and to leave everything in the hands of God. Now that you know this, I will teach you some techniques that will allow you to achieve the successful results quickly, but only after you have correctly defined point B.

First, you need to establish a proper way to formulate your objectives. Most of the people do not dedicate enough time to do this and that is a big mistake; unknowingly, when you do not plan for success you are planning for failure. The universe is constantly, twenty-four hours a day asking you this question: what do you want? And, whether you know it or not, your answer comes through your words and thoughts. When you first get up in the morning, you need to outline what the day will look like, and because of this, you also need to choose you words carefully. When you formulate your objectives, keep in mind you must establish your wishes in the first person, I, in present tense, NOW, and as an affirmation determining what you want, instead of knowing what you do not want.

Secure the ecology of your wishes, meaning, make sure your wishes are advantageous to you, to everyone and to nature. In other words, nobody, absolutely nobody must lose. Always establish win-win goals.

The following techniques help to accelerate the materialization of your successful results:

1. **Treasure mapping**: Build a vision board with a collage of images that represent what you desire; place on it what you want as if you already got it and take a picture of yourself in possession of what you desire. If you cut a picture from a magazine, put a picture of yourself next to it, but one where you look happy. Aim your dreams toward these seven important aspects of life:

    - Spiritual aspect: Place an image that connects you with the divine, with the thought in mind that you always expect the materialization of your dreams for the greatest good and the highest of ends. In other words, that the perfection and hand of God will guide the materialization of your dreams at the right moment and in the perfect way, according to God's divine will and grace.

    - Physical aspect: Place an image of a body that represents your ideal body type, or a picture of yours from the past when you had the body you would like to have now. If you cut the image from a magazine, place a picture of your face over the original face.

    - Relationships aspect: If you desire a love relationship, find a picture of the entire body of a person whose general treats resemble the aspects you would like your partner to have, place it on the vision board and next to it place a picture of yourself where you look fulfilled and happy. If what you desire is to have lots of friends, find a picture of a lot of people enjoying with each other and substitute the face in one of the bodies for yours, or place a picture of your entire body that matches the image.

- Educational aspect: Select an image of the place where you wish to study, the degree you wish to obtain and a picture of someone graduating who looks happy. It can also be a picture of something else you wish to learn, such as a sport, a technical degree, a language, playing an instrument or some form of plastic art. On this vision board, you may place the images of whatever you desire, just remember to place an image of yours or your face over the body of someone doing what you wish to learn, keeping in mind that you already know it.

- Occupational aspect: Place an image that represents how you would like to make a living. If you wish to work, find an image of the place where you wish to work and the picture of the company you would like to work for; your picture next to it showing your job title and how much you would like to earn in wages. If you were an entrepreneur, determine the kind of successful business you would like to have, the image of a board meeting showing you as the leader of it, announcing that you have surpassed all your goals. Remember to establish your monthly wages for running your own business.

- Economics aspect: Place images of the things you desire to have, such as your car or cars, your dream house, farm, plane, jewels, computers, clothes, etc. You may also add images of the restaurants you wish to go to, the people you would like to help, the comforts you would like to have at home or at your office, like refrigerators, living room, dining room, paintings, washer and dryer, TV, audio systems; absolutely everything you would like to have, but be careful what you wish for because everything materializes.

- Recreational aspect: Choose the places you wish to go to on vacations; you may choose to visit different places of the world. Place the images of each specific place for each country you wish to visit. Choose five star hotels and travel first class, as well as a picture of yours with the people you wish to travel with. You place the limits; to wish for something that is less than the best points to low self-esteem issues.

Give a title to your vision board, such as 'treasure map,' or any other name you want. Keep in mind you must not leave blank spaces in between pictures; the whole vision board must be filled and it does not matter in which order you place your dreams. Once it is ready, put it in front of your bed and make sure it is the last thing you look at before going to sleep, and the first thing you see when you wake up in the morning. When you look at your vision board, say the following prayer: *Thank you, Father, I know you have given the order for all of this to materialize in the right moment, according to your will, for the greatest good and the highest of purposes.* Take off the images that pertain to any dream that has already materialized and replace it for a new dream. Just looking at this vision board will fill you with energy to live your day to the fullest, one hundred percent.

– "Is it that easy?" I asked. "Just look at it and wait for the miracle to happen?"

– "Yes," he replied, "That is it. The 'how' to get what you want is left to the universe itself, to the one who created the day and night, the sun and the moon, the galaxies, nature, the mineral, vegetal and animal kingdoms; I am sure it will be very easy for Him to make your dreams come true. For now, be certain and have confidence, this is the key; it is important to make sure of what you are 'really' thinking because many times we think we are thinking and in reality someone else is thinking about us. Other times we live within the boundaries of the limitations that our parents have imposed on us at an unconscious level, of whatever they thought to be possible or not possible, right or wrong.

On occasions, I have been asked some of the following questions:

What will be the future of our armed forces?

What will be the future of this university? – The place where I was giving a conference.
What will be the future of my company? – A businessperson asked.

And to all I gave the same answer: None. Each one of their faces paled when they heard my surprising answer; then, I made it clear that the right thing was to create the armed forces of the future, the University of the Future and the business of the future.

Although apparently there was no difference, in reality there was, and a big one: in the first case, you are only reproducing thoughts being thought by others, it is to live through today's paradigms; in the second place, it is going to the future to observe everything from that perspective, beyond the limits of time, money and all paradigms. This in turn, makes unlimited creators out of us and that is to think, to create.

If you get used to going to the future and thinking how you would like to live there, and then come back to the present and execute the necessary moves in order to arrive to that future you have created, then you are co-creating with God and you are waking up from the hypnosis that leads you to believe changes must happen in slow and progressive moves. In reality, space, time and speed limits are set by us as creators. To God, it is the same now or a century from now; easy or difficult, a little or too much, expensive or cheap; those obstacles are a part of our intellect. To believe is to create, so be clear about the details of what you want.

Do not fall in the trap of being too general; the desire to travel is not enough, you must determine where to, when, with whom, for how long, staying at which hotel, with which airline. You do the same when you envision the house of your dreams. Do not limit the creation by merely saying, 'I want to buy a house,' because maybe you just wish to own a house and it does not matter whether you buy it, if it is given to you as a gift or if you win it in a raffle. Do not limit the way your dream may come true. For example, you do not wish to have a million dollars no matter what, for surely you do not want to receive it as a result of collecting a relative's life insurance policy; nor do you want to lose ten pounds whatever the cost, lest you lose a limb on an accident. Be wise in your creations; take care of generalizations and always observe the ecology of your wishes. A good formula to accomplish it is through shifting your perspective; in other words, to go from being the one who begs, to the one who makes dreams come true. Think about it this way, *'if someone else was asking me for this, in how many ways could I interpret the request?'* Make sure you are being clear and precise."

— "You mentioned there are several techniques to quickly materialize our successful results. Which techniques are these?" I asked him.

— "Let us go slowly." He said. "Today you will learn seven of them, and they will be more than enough to help you materialize your deepest desires and dreams."

2. **Objectives board**: make a display board and write down your dreams in the first person and as an affirmation, with the exact date when you wish to accomplish each one of your dreams and adding empowering words that will boost your levels of enthusiasm and happiness.

For example:

"On this day, Monday, November 15th of ————, I, ————, feel absolutely happy for having achieved ————————————————————."

Your display board must have seven affirmations corresponding to each one of the seven aspects I mentioned to you before. It will be much more effective if the font color is red and the background is yellow; this will make it reach your unconscious and fix it deep in every time you see it, and as a result, it will support the materialization of your dreams when and how you want them to. Place this display board in your room as well, in a place where you can read it right after having had your attention on your treasure map.

3. **The power of imagination:** Select a comfortable place in your house or office and dedicate thirty minutes of your day to the art of creating. Do this every day, and if you desire, you may light a candle and invoke the light of God who never fails.

– "How do you invoke the light of God?" I asked.

– "You only need to say this, 'Lord, I invoke your light for the greater good and the highest of ends, so that what I create with this visualization may materialize under your grace and in perfect manner. Thank you, Father, who listens to me.' And with that, you have invoked he light.

When you begin your visualization process, first and foremost, sit on a comfortable chair or sofa, close your eyes, count from ten to one and imagine that you are coming down a stair way as you descend through each number, step by step. Feel your body and mind relax and become more and more at peace. Relax your breathing and pay attention to how you slowly inhale and exhale, and when you get to number one, you should be completely relaxed. Then, bring your attention to the middle of the brain; you may do this by giving the mental order for your thoughts to go there, like when you think about your stomach, your left foot or any other part of your body. Once you hear a kind of whisper in the middle of your brain – like the kind produced by the wind – give the order to your blood to flow with more intensity in this place; this will elevate the quality and quantity of your energy, and will bring more oxygen to the brain.

Image a white light descending from the highest places of the universe and see how it envelops you; then, with the peace brought forth by the knowingness that God is supporting you, begin to visualize yourself – like in a movie – with movement, in colors and seeing yourself as the main character, and that you already achieved your dream. Involve all your senses as much as you can. Look around you and see everything bright and clear; observe all the details using your imagination. See yourself being congratulated by your friends because you obtained what you deeply desired. Listen to the whisper of the wind, the clapping of the hands, perceive the smells of the place where you are and relate it to something very pleasant. In your mind, touch what you have created and experience how it feels; manifest happiness, laughter and enthusiasm, feel the embrace of someone who truly is with you; feel the sensation of grasping each other's hands; imagine a flavor that connects you with that creation, such as coffee, water or some fruit juice. Become aware of the small details in your surroundings, visualizing a warm atmosphere and that you are the main character in that creation. Associate yourself with the experience as much as you can.

Some people complain they cannot see anything, the reason being very simple: we all have five senses, but some have certain senses more developed than others. Some people are visual; others are auditory, while others are more kinesthetic. Hence, do not worry, just enjoy imagining with the help of whatever sense of yours is more developed; get all your senses involved to the max. Remember: the more, the better. Do not imagine the process or how you will obtain the result, just focus on the outcome, the successful result; and when you are finished with your creative session, give thanks knowing that it will materialize in the right moment and place.

Remember to pay attention to how you feel, because that is the key to knowing whether we are creating in perfection or not. If something bothers you, ask yourself why and you will see that the answer will come through you. With each passing day, trust your intuition more and more for it is the voice of God. Be happy, as if the universe already received your order and nothing, no one can take you from the conquest of such perfect creation. Give thanks with the certainty that it is real and keep your creation to yourself, do not share your visualization with anybody. On one hand, being silent will help you focus all your energy in your creation, and on the other hand, because you do not know what lies in the heart or mind of the person you are sharing with, nor do you know the limits of what is possible of not for that person. As such, it is best you do not share with anybody, not even with your own family, in this way you will also begin to get used to talking about results and not about the processes.

When you finish your visualization, count from one to ten, and with each number you climb a step; as you go up the stairway, feel the rhythm of your breath and the flow of your blood begin to normalize. Feel the muscles of your body; open your eyes and by the time you are fully aware of your body you should be in the tenth step up the stairway, filled with energy and enthusiasm."

– "What if my mind begins to fill with doubt during the rest of the day?" I asked. "What should I do then?"

– "To handle doubt is pretty easy; you just need to fill yourself with enough evidence to the contrary, whether through information or experiences. When doubt fills your mind, just remind yourself that God is in charge and your dreams will come true before you can even imagine. You do the same when the storyteller comes into play. It will happen many times, because we all have this internal little voice that either plants doubt in our minds or brings our focus away from what we desire by creating new fantasies that, in the majority of the cases, may seem to be related to what we want but are only draining our energy."

–"Storyteller?" I wondered.

– "Yes," Said Mr. Deeb. "The storyteller is that internal little voice that distracts us, and it is in charge of driving our focus away by presenting us with disempowering alternatives and robbing us of the time we have set aside to visualize our successful result. These fantasies usually speak about the process; about how we will obtain what we want: yes, you desire to prosper, and the way to do it is by improving your performance at work, getting a promotion or, if you are paid by performance, by becoming more productive. Your focus is to see yourself already in point B, having achieved your promotion or increased your performance. You must consecrate the necessary amount of time you need in order to visualize your successful result; to make it even more effective, dedicate at least thirty minutes every day and do not allow the deceiving story teller to distract you. As you educate your internal story teller, by focusing, persevering and keeping your attention only on what you desire, this character becomes another one of your great attributes."

4. **Decrees:** Our words have power and we become what we speak of; words are the seeds we spread in the field of possibilities, the place where everything is possible. Limits do not exist, and the fruit we receive is precisely equal to what we sowed with our words. Our words will forge the reality of our world; when we choose the words that come out of our mouths, we are choosing our future.

The Bible says the following: 'In the beginning was the word and the word was with God, and the word was God. The same was in the beginning with God. All things were made by Him; and without Him was not anything made that was made. In Him was life: and the life was the light of men.' Many times as kids we were taught proper oral hygiene, but we were never taught proper verbal hygiene. We do not realize that when we say something, kidding or not, eventually those words will materialize.

To affirm, decree something, is to express in a loud voice what we desire as if we already got it; we say it in first person, present tense and as a decree. The following are some examples:

- I am ——————— ———————, "the best, the owner, the happy one, or whatever you wish to achieve" of ——————— ———————————————————————————.

- I am the best sales man of ——————— "company's name or product's name."

- I am a slender, healthy and happy person.

- I am connected to the wealth of the Universe. Money flows to me legally, constantly, easily and in abundance.

- Every day and in every way, I am better, better and better.

- I thoroughly enjoy my love relationship, and I guide my children toward the fulfillment of the mission for which they have been created.

- I constantly manifest the purpose of my life from the light of my heart.

- God is with me now and He always guides me.

- I am a successful professional, graduated from the University of ⎯⎯⎯⎯⎯⎯, as a ⎯⎯⎯⎯⎯⎯.

- I enjoy fifteen days of vacations in ⎯⎯⎯⎯⎯⎯⎯, in the company of ⎯⎯⎯⎯⎯⎯⎯, traveling first class and staying at five star hotels.

You can take these affirmations as an example in order to make your own. Remember, creativity is infinite and you may even create internal qualities, such as humility, perseverance, constancy, responsibility, patience, honesty; and external qualities as well, such as: job performance, achieving an objective or the acquisition of a piece of real estate.

Repeat these decrees out lout, a thousand times a day, when you get up in the morning, in the shower, while driving, before falling asleep; repeat them at all times. The more often you say your decrees, the better. Fill your mind with that decree until you can say it without having to think about it, automatically, like saying your name. Do this for forty days in a row; you do not need to believe, just do it and you will see how the magic of the world will manifest in you every day, and what seems impossible to achieve today will be possible tomorrow. Do it! Some studies have determined that decrees materialize faster if you repeat them during your sleep.

– "During my sleep?" I inquired.

– "Yes," He said, "let us assume you go to sleep at 11 pm at night and wake up at 6 am in the morning; that is your sleeping schedule. It will be most effective if you say your decrees from 11 pm to 12 am and from 5 am to 6 am, when you are half-asleep, because you enter a level of brainwave known as alpha waves, and at this level, you are able to connect with your subliminal sphere. In that sleepy state, your creations reach your unconscious mind more rapidly, which in turn helps your dreams materialize faster. You do not need to feel or analyze what you are saying, just repeat it. You will be amazed to see how this information will infiltrate the part of your mind that never sleeps and enjoys bringing miracles into your life. Your mind has several spheres, and each one of them records different experiences."

– "What are these spheres?" I asked Mr. Deeb.

– "They are seven: the preconscious, subconscious, conscious, continuous consciousness, supra consciousness and akashic record. The subconscious and subliminal contain the information that propels your involuntary reactions, meaning, the ones you cannot even understand. This is the place that records all the publicity, which manages to have an impact when it successfully involves your five senses and it is repeated several times; this is the creation and presentation mechanism, so those who work in publicity know that the more the better. As a result, if one is not conscious of this, one will have an automatic response after having listened to several repetitions of the same suggestion to drink a certain type of soda, try a certain food or buy a certain product. With this course, you are learning to program yourself consciously at that level so no one can externally manipulate you. You will follow our own orders."

– "Do I say the decrees out loud or in my head?"

– "Out loud," He replied, "because when you say them in your head you do not get the words but the images; I already taught you the way to create with images."

– "Should I focus on what I am saying then?" I asked again.

– "Not necessarily. If you just repeat them a certain number of times, throughout the course of those forty days, it will be more than enough. You can be sure that what you decree will come true."

– "But, why forty days and a thousand times?" I questioned.

– "I will explain it in the future, not now. For the moment, I assure you the way I have explained it to you will work; just do it so you can confirm it on your own. The numbers have a reason to be; there was a specific reason Jesus Christ fasted for forty days and forty nights, and God guided Moses and his people through the desert for forty years. But just to please your intellect, I will say that forty and a thousand are numbers for closing cycles, to complete creations, as a result, you can assume they are finalized. I assure you, at least a thousand times a day, never less than that; the more the better. On the other hand, if you fall asleep repeating it, it will record it in the deepest parts of your unconscious mind, which will help materialize your desire even faster. The forty days are precisely that, forty days; no more and no less. Another powerful way to do it is by looking at yourself in the mirror as you repeat your affirmations, a thousand times, nonstop; this might be the most effective way to do it. When you end this cycle, you may begin a new one with a different decree about something else you wish to create.

You, as a whole identity, are a spiritual being experiencing the material. The part of you that gives you the energy to live, work and enjoy, is what some people call the *basic being*. That basic being must be cared for like you care for a child and you have to make deals with him; for example: today, I will work the whole day and then rest at night, or I will go to the movies, or enjoy a good party or dinner. The basic being will be pleased to receive anything that will bring joy to his day, and he will give you the energy you need at every moment. However, never make yourself a promise you do not intend to fulfill, otherwise that basic being will sabotage your dreams inviting you to delay things or making you feel like you have no energy. When you promise something to yourself, do it or do not make any promises.

When you give thanks to God, it is the spiritual being made manifest through you; when you analyze something, it is the mental being that manifests; and that part of you that likes comfort and fun is the basic being. You can also see yourself as having three facets: a child, an adult and a father; the child likes to have fun, the adult prefers to be responsible, and the father likes to guide, order you around and judge. The most important thing is that every person needs to assume the role that is pertinent to each moment.

The basic being is there to support or sabotage you, depending on whether it feels it is being taken into consideration or not. For example: if you start a forty day period of decrees and you promise yourself that in the end you will reward yourself with something that excites you, your basic being – focusing on the reward – will give you the energy you need in order to finish the task so it can enjoy the reward. If you do not promise any kind of reward, the basic being will feel unnoticed, not stimulated, and as a result, the self-sabotage will prevent you from finishing your objectives with success.

Every person of success that recognizes this process understands they need to do two things before embarking upon a new project so it can end in a successful result: they establish a price that is enticing enough to provide the energy they need in order to drive them all the way to the end result. As soon as a person sets a goal for himself, some sort of obstacle appears that is directly proportional to the task at hand. Those who know about this mechanism do not allow themselves to be put down by it, by the appearance of doubt and skepticism; on the contrary, they set their minds on achieving their goal, recognizing that the most important thing in the pursuit of their dream is not to conquer the external, but to conquer themselves.

At the end of the forty days, when you are done with a cycle of decrees, it is important to rest before beginning a new cycle. You may pause for a week. When you begin a new cycle, decree the seven aspects we have talked about before, but do not repeat the same decrees you did before, for what you have created will materialize in its proper time and place. For example, if your previous decree was about prosperity, continue with health.

One day you will have the confidence of Jesus Christ and you will not need a thousand or forty in order to create something; maybe just saying it one time will be enough to make it come true. For now, live the processes of someone who is awakening and realizing he is not the victim of circumstances but the creator of his destiny, and in this state, you must take action. Only applied knowledge persists in the spirit, but please, do not believe my words, just DO IT.

Another potent way to decree is by involving different aspects of your life that make you deserving of obtaining the result. For example, let us assume you wish to become the manager of the company you work for; these would be very potent affirmations:

> I am the manager of ——————————————.
>
> I think like all managers of successful companies think.
>
> I live like all managers of successful companies live.
>
> I speak like managers of successful companies speak.
>
> I see like managers of successful companies see.
>
> I dress like managers of successful companies dress.
>
> I eat like managers of successful companies eat.
>
> I act like managers of successful companies act.
>
> I listen like managers of successful companies do.
>
> I feel like managers of successful companies feel.

I could continue to add more and more qualities that will allow you to believe your dreams are already true. Now, let us imagine you wish to be a millionaire; your decrees would be as follow:

> I am a millionaire.
>
> I act like a millionaire.
>
> I walk like a millionaire.
>
> I feel like a millionaire.

> I speak like a millionaire.
>
> I eat like a millionaire.
>
> I see like a millionaire.
>
> I dress like a millionaire.
>
> I am acquainted to the same people millionaires are.
>
> I think like a millionaire.
>
> I live like a millionaire.

Repeat these decrees repeatedly during the day, and whenever possible repeat them in front of a mirror.

5. **The power of mantras:** A mantra is a sound that, when continuously repeated, generates a frequency of vibration that makes you attractive or receptive to its meaning. For example, your name is a mantra. Unlike decrees, mantras can be said aloud or in your head, being more powerful when repeated in your head. Some people call the act of repeating mantras in your head and in a state of relaxation a spiritual practice, because they are conscious that when they repeat these, they create a sacred frequency that brings them closer to the divine.

In the Far East, the great-enlightened masters are used to giving one or several mantras to their disciples in order to establish a spiritual connection between them, the disciples and God. Some religious ceremonies would have people sing a mantra aloud with the purpose of creating group energy in alignment with the spirit. In some other cases, the master has a pool of mantras at his disposal from which he gives to the disciples, one at a time; following his own criteria, the master gives them more and more powerful mantras as he considers the disciples are ready for it. Te purpose being to bring the disciple closer and closer to being consciously aware of the soul, in communion with God and focused on the Divine.

You may create your own mantras by turning yourself at once into your own master teacher and disciple. Some will connect you with the spirit, others with the mental or the material. For example, if you wish to attract wealth into your life, you may mentally repeat the word WEALTH as many times as possible and as a form of whisper; it is effective to repeat your mantra before falling asleep and when you wake up. You may use your mantras with words like love, health, happiness, or any other quality you wish to materialize in your life.

The word OM is a mantra that puts you in alignment with the spirit and unites you with the powers of God; in English it translates to, I AM; as such, the more you say the expression I AM, the quicker that it will manifest in your life.

6. **Affirmations**: Affirmations are recordings that we encode in our cellular memory, turning us into a magnet to whatever we have recorded. The majority of people do not get what they want because they do not feel they deserve it. Affirmations help better their self-image, self-esteem and sense of worth, so they can continuously attract into their lives whatever they desire. The way to do it is very simple:

Take a sheet of paper and divide it into two vertical sections; the first section should take about seventy percent of the sheet and the second one will take the remaining thirty percent. Create a phrase that says what you wish to program your cells with, for example:

> I am happy.
>
> I deserve to be happy.
>
> I love and accept myself just as I am.
>
> I am the creator of my results.
>
> I am healthy and slender.
>
> I deserve to be wealthy.
>
> I make more money than I need.
> I am free.

I am prosperous.

I forgive———————— for ————————————————.

I forgive myself for ————————————————.

I feel the presence of God at this very moment.

I am an excellent apprentice.

I am an extraordinary disciple.

I am honest.

I am humble.

I am capable.

I attract people who accept and love me just as I am.

You must do these examples in the first person, as an affirmation and in present tense; they should be as short as possible.

Once you have chosen an affirmation for the exercise, take the part of the sheet that takes seventy percent of it and write it on it. Make sure you breathe in deep and feel every word as you do it; on the remaining thirty percent of the sheet of paper, write down the feelings or thoughts that come up as an immediate reaction as you write down the affirmation. Write down the affirmation seventy times along with its corresponding reaction. Once you are finished with this conscious writing process, take another sheet of paper and transform each one of the reactions into a phrase that reflects the opposite to what you felt or thought in response to your affirmation; only do it if the reaction was a negative one. When you finish the exercise, burn the sheets of paper so you can transmute into light what you wrote in them.

Do this exercise for seven days in a row. I will give you here an example:

1. I am happy...	but I have many debts
2. I am happy...	nobody loves me
3. I am happy...	and people notice it
4. I am happy...	but I feel ugly
5. I am happy...	etc

After you write down your affirmation seventy times, proceed to change the answers to the remaining thirty percent of the sheet.

1- The universe provides me with all I need.

2- Everyone I know loves and accepts me just as I am.

3- «Do not write anything on this line because the reaction was a positive one»

4- I am a beautiful, unique and special being.

Once you finish this cycle of seven days, you may begin with a new affirmation that you wish to program your cells with.

— "What is a cycle?" I asked Mr. Deeb.

— "It is an energetic process with three stages: You start something, you develop it and then you end it. It is to start and finish something, completing a task all the way to its end. To write down the affirmation seventy times, every day for seven days in a row is a cycle; and before you ask, let me tell you that seventy and seven are also sacred numbers. Remember the Christ inviting us to forgive seventy seven times.

Other types of affirmations are done through hypnosis. Every time you get all five senses involved in order to give or receive information, you are hypnotizing or being hypnotized. In your mind, grab a lime and take a good look at its green color, squeeze it hard, smell it, hit it against your other hand

and listen to the sound it makes. Then, with an imaginary knife, cut it in half, look at its seeds and observe its juices running down your hand; do all of this in your mind. If your eyes were closed, open them up; if you did what I said, you should have salivated more than usual, although as you could see the lime does not exist, is just a part of your imagination. This is a common form of hypnosis. The genius minds in the advertising industry make great use of hypnosis as a means to make people believe they really need a product or service. If you observe closely, you will realize their attempts at getting all your senses involved to the maximum."

– "And, how does this apply to the subject of creating potent affirmations?" I wondered.

– "Let us see." He said. "Stand up in front of a mirror. If you look straight at your face, you will involve the sense of sight. Take a deep breath before you say your affirmation and your will be using your sense of smell. Repeat your affirmation aloud to engage the auditory sense. Make sure your hands are touching some part of your body in order to anchor yourself, like joining your hands or placing them over your heart, your forehead or any other part of your body that you choose. With that, you will be activating the sense of touch. Feel the saliva in your mouth, and if it is necessary, drink some liquid in order to engage your sense of taste. All of this allows you to program yourself through self-hypnosis, which in turn changes your cellular memory.

With regards to affirmations for self-hypnosis, do not worry about how many times you repeat them, just remember that the more the better."

– "Which, among all of these techniques, is the most powerful?" I asked.

– "That is a fair question, and the answer is: the one that suits you better. Just remember that the more the better. Each time you do it, you will become increasingly aware of the number of times that works for you, according to the results you get."

7. **The power of our connection to the Divine:** This might be the most potent way to bring into your life exactly whatever

it is you desire. To feel connected to the source is to feel alive, with purpose and filled with energy; the more connection you experience, the less limitation that you have. You will learn to trust more and will differentiate between two types of events that may come into your life: centripetal events, or people and events that come to you without you having to look for them; and centrifugal events, or people and events that you look for.

When you are connected with the source, what happens to you makes sense in the Divine plan. The people and events that come into your life are the way God answers to your prayers, and these are known as centripetal. It is good to wake up to the understanding that nothing happens by chance, but rather as causality. People who live their lives asleep, do not realize these people and events happening in their lives hold the answers to their requests; because of this, they become more diligent in their search for it on the outside; they ignore the fact that the more connected you are, the more effective is the work you do from the inside. It is a matter of attracting and allowing in order for the answer to come.

There are four ways to achieve your connection to the Divine, and those are prayer, meditation, spiritual exercises and contemplation. Let us explain each one of them:

PRAYER

To pray is to talk to God. It is, according to your own feelings and in your own words, having a frank and sincere talk with the almighty. The best way to pray is to give thanks for what has been given, and if you are a man or woman of faith, you need to learn to give thanks for what has yet to be given. An adequate form of prayer would be the following: 'Thank you, Lord, for what you have given to me and for what you have yet to give to me, thank you, Lord.'

When you breathe you become connected, the question is, to what?
To the light or the shadow; to limitations or the unlimited; each breath programs you. It is good to understand the types

of programs you are creating in yourself; live your life inhaling good news, and constantly breathe in deep so that each and every day your life fills up with more happiness. It is also convenient to turn God into your partner, and live turning the lights on at every moment of your life. This is the mandate we have received for our first day in creation, when we know we are co-creators with God and consistently separate the light from the darkness, helping us to avoid many problems and to travel light, enjoying the passing of our days.

Scientific prayer always works, and with it you will get the answers to your requests; it is divided into three parts: The first part is to give thanks; people who are known to be spiritual dedicate as much time as possible to this stage. Some people complain their prayers are not heard, but they fail to see they go through this stage too quickly. The second part is to invoke Divine will. It is to say that, above and beyond your desires, you accept the will of God and declare that all your dreams are for the greatest good and the highest of ends; that any dream you may have will be subordinated to the will of the one who can do it all and knows all, the will of God. The third part is your request, being this part the least important because God knows exactly what you need, yet this is the part where people spend the most time.

When you talk to God through prayer, even if you have yet to receive what your heart desires, there is a sense of fulfillment, acceptance and enthusiasm that springs from within and which are difficult to describe. Let your life be a continuous prayer, an ovation of thanks and a strong willed decision to leave all your thoughts, words and deeds in the hands of God. Remember: pray and do.

Meditation

Meditation is the act of listening to God, and there are many types of meditation. For example, there is light, water, fire, nature, sound, and creative meditations; and then some others are mantra yoga meditation and transcendental meditation. The form of meditation is not important, but the result. As such, you must make sure the style you follow helps to fulfill the purpose of listening to God, and with it, discovering the purpose of your heart so it may be made manifest for its glory.

Regardless of the meditation style you choose, remember well the concept of the tithe: dedicate ten percent of your day, every day, to be in contact with the Creator; do it in whichever way you choose, as with practice you will realize this is the key to humanity's happiness and sense of fulfillment. If you do not have enough time to be in communication with God and leave things in His hands, then for sure you will have the time to live immersed in problems and not knowing the best way to solve them.

– "Two hours and forty minutes in meditation is a lot of time! At what time do I do everything else?" I asked surprised.

– "Not just meditating," He said, "you may spend some of that time praying, meditating, doing spiritual exercises and contemplating. Besides, you may distribute this time throughout the day. If you analyze the happiest people you know, you will find a common thread to all of them: they dedicate the greatest part of their time to God.

Spiritual exercises

I have already talked to you about the spiritual exercises. They help to create movement toward God in order to walk consciously back to the soul, and this is achieved through the repetition of a mantra given by a spiritual teacher of Light at the moment of initiation. This initiation is a ritual created to make the delivery of the mantra a special moment. You repeat the mantra after invoking the light, usually accompanied by the lighting of a candle so the fire will transmute any kind of unbalance or negative energy that may be released during the process. The mantra is repeated aloud when it is done collectively, but you say it mentally if it is a personalized mantra.

Spiritual mantras seek to lead the one who repeats them ever closer to the soul, back to the place where we all come from, in order to bring into alignment our energetic body and fields with the highest frequency of light we can sustain, thus fulfilling the will of God on Earth.

Contemplation

Many Churches use contemplation, and it consists on seeing God through sacred images or in perfection. Now I would like to give you a higher level of contemplation: See God in the eyes of every person that comes your way, in every mineral, vegetable or animal; see God around you and beyond the concepts of good and bad, see God even if what you are seeing does not seem right to you. See God in every experience that you live.

Contemplate God at every moment; elevate yourself and do not allow yourself to be trapped by the illusions of form. Remember, it is impossible to be separate from God, the all who is contained in everything and each and every part of it. See beyond the surface of the skin and connect to the heart of things, and then you will be connecting to God.

Another potent way to enjoy contemplation is by means of perceiving the Christ within. Jesus Christ came to teach us how to find that energy which connects us to the spirit through our hearts. In order to contemplate the Christ within, visualize a sun within your heart and feel it moving clockwise; this is the Christ energy that is in every human being. Many die without knowing of its existence, and worse, without the understanding that this energy connects us to the Creator and all its power. Practice this simple exercise and you will be amazed as to how powerful it is. When you visualize your Christ within, tell Him all about your problems and whatever solutions you think might apply, and then give thanks for being in charge of your creations so they can materialize in perfect time; after that, have the patience to wait and you will experience extraordinary results.

When you learn to connect with the Christ energy you will surely learn to perform miracles; remember what Jesus Christ once said: 'I am the way, the truth and the life. No one comes to the Father except through me.' The Father is God, and the Son is the Christ within everyone one of us and with whom we need to develop a close relationship in order to get to the Father.

– "Is there some sort of prerequisite to make the communication more effective?" I wondered

– "Yes," Mr. Deeb answered, "in order to fully activate your Christ energy you need to first and foremost forgive and accept yourself unconditionally; in other words, love yourself. Invoke the forgiveness of those whom you hurt in thought, word, deed or by omission, whether you remember it or no; then, send your forgiveness to those who hurt you in thought, word, deed or by omission, whether you remember it or not. Invoke the memory of the days and free yourself."

– "How does one do this invocation?"

– "Just be very clear in your statement that you love yourself unconditionally, and that you forgive yourself for any self-judgment or judgments toward others. Tell God that you request the forgiveness of all the people you may have hurt in thought, word, deed or by omission; whether you remember it or not, and that you send your forgiveness to all those who hurt you in thought, word, deed or by omission, whether you remember it or not. Then, visualize the light of a candle at the center of the sun and ask whatever you desire, because, believe it or not, right at that moment you are talking to God.

Do this and then tell me what happens; this is a foolproof formula, is just that very few people use it. You need to live in Christ, be yourself a living Christ, and one day you will be able to manifest the glory of the One who came before you. Remember, He said if we believed we would be able to do greater things than He did. People are waiting for the second coming of Christ, and this will happen to those who learn to connect with Him through their hearts.

Many of us have heard the phrase, 'search for Christ within your heart,' yet very few have managed to establish the real meaning of it. Now, the antichrist is anyone who denies a place for Christ in their hearts and for the living Christ in others.

When your level of consciousness allows it, and through contemplation activate your Christ energy making you a living Christ, I will be perfectly capable of calling you by your name and then add the word 'Christ' to it. People could say: there goes John the Christ, Peter the Christ, Mary the Christ, or whatever the name of those who achieve this level of consciousness. At that moment, your body will be the temple and you will not need to go anywhere in order to connect to the Divine; your connection to God will be 24/7 and you will learn to live in His light and make decision with Him. All intermediaries between you and Him will lose their power and you will live a practical spiritual life. Become a warrior of the light."

– "How can I attain this?" I asked him.

– "In the Genesis," Mr. Deeb continued. "The Bible establishes that on the first day of creation God separated light from darkness. You become a warrior of the light when you live life continually separating the light from your own darkness. It is very simple to achieve: invoke the light when you get up so God may illuminate your day; do the same when you take food, and you will notice your body begins to attract only the foods that are nourishing and convenient to its countenance. Invoke the light before you begin the day's labor, before making a new decision, before relating to a person, before you begin a new project, when you go to bed; invoke the light at every new moment of the day. This is what it means to be a warrior of the light.

At the beginning, you are like a matchstick whose light can be lit and extinguished very quickly; little by little, the light grows into your life until it turns into a great torch, illuminating the lives of those who come your way or the places where you go. Imagine a white light coming from way up above, as high above as you can imagine, coming from beyond the sun and the stars, and then say: 'I invoke the light of God for the greater good and the highest of ends,' and so you are in the light."

Discipline and discernment

In order to be a disciple of the Light, you must have the two most important treats of any disciple: discipline and discernment. You can achieve Discipline by educating yourself to fulfill small promises to your own self and to others.

External discipline

In the process of forging your character, you need external sources of discipline imposed on you in order to support your formation. At the beginning, your parents set limits and give you responsibilities. Then, when you are in school, you are given a class schedule, homework, tests and so on; later on as you are working, your boss or employer tells you at what time you clock in, when to take a break, how much money you make and what you have to do. In other words, you are conditioned by the external orders, decisions and parameters you have been given; you have no control over your life and you are moved to the tune of whoever is imparting their discipline on you.

External discipline will help you to live according to a pre-established set of norms, and it is the previous step to acquiring internal discipline. Discipline sets you free, and you are a slave in those areas where you have no discipline.

Internal discipline

As you continue forging your character, you stop needing having someone telling you what to do, how to do it and when to do it, and you begin to do what is necessary out of your own volition. This kind of discipline is what makes businessmen, leaders, people that others want to follow; these individuals are noteworthy because they treasure their word and only commit to what they know they can fulfill; in turn, they easily gain the respect of others.

This kind of discipline is achieved by conquering yourself, determining the current state of your life for each one of the seven aspects (column A) and where you wish to be (column B), verifying that each step given brings you closer to the place you have established, the place you wish to arrive to. This kind of discipline makes you more competent and effective at achieving the external results you desire.

Levels of transformation through acceptance and discipline:

Levels	How I am today	How I wish to be and when
Spiritual		
Physical		
Relationships		
Educational		
Occupational		
Financial		
Recreational		

Draw a table where you clearly detail how you feel today in each one of those seven levels, and how you would like to be in a year from now. Do not worry about how you are going to achieve it because you will learn this later on; for now, the most important thing is to establish this parallel between where you are and where you want to be.

To create the habit of knowing where you are and where you want to be is the first step to begin applying the principles of success in your life. In the physical aspect, for example, you could write down how you are today without any kid of judgments, just describing the reality of your body: you are healthy or sick, your muscles are rigid or flaccid; you act lethargic or normal, you have some extra pounds or the right weight for you. Then, write down what you desire to have or be in the future and on a specific date, such as a slender person, agile, flexible, healthy, and that you wish to weigh a certain amount of pounds.

Set your goals beyond your existing limits, knowing that anything is possible. The more precise your description of the successful result you desire is, the easier it will be to achieve it. Do the same with each one of the seven levels. Character is forged by choosing beyond our wishes and momentary distractions, so that every step will lead you from where you are to where you desire to be. Coherence is not the state in which you think, speak and act all in alignment and in the same direction, for if that was true we would all be incoherent for the most part. This is why I invite you to think of coherence in terms of making every step one that takes you from where you are, to the place you want to be.

Spiritual discipline

The highest level of character is when you have acquired the discipline to make the will of God in this planet and follow His lead whether you like it or not. It is the kind of discipline that makes a Jesus Christ be willing to die in the cross for the love of humanity; a Mother Theresa of Calcutta to be completely dedicated to helping the terminally ill in their process of passing from this plane and going back to Father; a Saint John to have the patience needed to pass any test no matter how difficult, knowing it is Divine will; a Moses to spend forty years leading the people of Israel through the dessert, no matter the struggle; a Gandhi to, through prayer and fast, gain that independence of India.

This is the kind of discipline that pushes you on a daily basis to fulfill the purpose for which you were created; giving thanks for every event, leaving everything in the hands of God and being willing to do His will, seeing every problem as an opportunity to grow, to be, learning to trust in the eternal. Perhaps the most important thing in this life is to attain spiritual discipline.

Discipline helps you to make constant responsible choices in every aspect of your life. Responsibility tells you that you are where you are because of what you have done or not done. It saves you from losing time if you are trying to learn from someone who only teaches with words; it shows you that many people want to recruit you, force you to follow them only because they think they are right or they have the perfect formula. When you are a true disciple, you only learn from the one who has achieved the result you desire, and you learn from that person the strategy that led them to their results. It is very common to see people following individuals who are themselves lost. The formula to avoid falling in such a trap is to learn from those who have achieved the successful result; hence, you must determine the exact strategy that they used.

Discernment

Discernment is the capacity to choose consciously the proper path to go from where you are to where you want to be, and discipline is the first treat of a warrior of the light, discernment is the second most important quality needed to avoid getting lost in the spiritual path.

You must never surrender your capacity to discern, lest you get lost on the way and end up being a follower or a servant to a false leader; a true leader focuses on making a new leader out of the disciple. Discernment is not applied to the concepts of good and bad, for this is only a deceiving game played by our inner judge in its effort to make us feel like we know it all; instead, it must be applied to what you think is right, in other words, what brings you farther or closer to your desires."

– "This may sound like quite the crude conclusion," I said, "but this is what I understand from what you are saying: I can do whatever I want, whatever rocks my world in order to fulfill my desires, is that correct?"

– "Yes," he answered, "for as long as you are living in the light or grace, and not under the law."

– "What is the difference?"

– "You live in the light or grace when both your actions and your wishes are for the greater good and the highest of ends, meaning, when every person involved wins; when the ecology of your dreams has been properly established so you may create without falling prey to doubts. You live under the law when someone else has to lose so that you may win. In this case, eventually you will realize you lost as well, because in the end you will know that whatever you do under the law comes back to you. It is very common to see people getting lost because they gave up their discernment. They gave up their power to a pseudo-leader who managed to trick them by means of his words; or maybe they forgot to chew on the mental nourishment they received and ended up swallowing the information as a whole, which in some cases is full of viruses or false premises. When you look at it from the perspective of the path to success, these kinds of situations push you farther away from what you desire.

In the art of discernment you do not need to enter into an argument, you need only make a conscious choice between the information you receive and what is truly convenient for you. Remember, even though people may be right for the most part, in some circumstances they may be wrong or may unknowingly give you information that detours you from the path that takes you to the place you have already chosen; they may honestly be wrong without them even knowing. The more you believe in a person, or the more you respect him, the more discernment you need, for you are in danger of swallowing the whole chunk and end up taking false information as correct, only because someone you believe in told you about it or because many people believe the same. Do you think that spiritual leader who invited his followers to commit suicide in order to be saved did it out of malice? He probably did not; maybe he was honestly wrong and did not realize it.

Here is another piece of homework for you: Invoke the support of Christ within when you need to discern and choose the proper kind of information, and leave in His hands whatever it is you desire. I want you to pay close attention to how you feel and what happens around you when you choose to be a warrior of the light."

– "I have received a lot of information," I interjected in a low voice, meditating on what I had lived throughout the whole interview, which I do not even know how long it lasted because it was very late by the time I left, "I have a feeling I have a lot to understand."

I usually lost all sense of time whenever I was with him, it was as if time went by very quickly; but more than tired I felt excited with so much information, like I had received a special gift from life. I wonder how many people would want to have such an experience! When did I earn the right to it? Why all of this information? And, just for me? Why not turn it into a workshop and teach it to others? Or maybe record it at a studio or give up his decision to live without writing a book? These and many more thoughts meandered in my mind, and the storyteller distracted me for a while until his voice brought me back to the present moment.

– "Yes," He replied, "so chew it all very well, analyze it, try to prove it right or wrong, let your discernment be your companion; do not believe what I have said. Only if it sounds logical, apply it and prove that its application connects you to what you desire; do not rush because there is nowhere to go. Next week we will continue with the second part to the road of success. I hope you meditate on what you have just learned today, and let any doubt or comment be a part of our next discussion. Think about the next important thing on this route, if you are clear about it, you will become conscious of something of utmost importance for your future. Oh! It is important for you to know there are three practices that will assist you in the conquering of your successful result, if you wish to materialize them faster.

1. Focus: Put your attention on what you want, and what you do not want will disappear from your life; in the direction that you look to is where you will go; focus on the impossible and the possible will come true. The bigger the problem the smaller the dream, the greater the dream the smaller the problem; impossible dreams have zero problems. Everything that is possible today was thought to be impossible at some point in the past.

2. Gratefulness: Give thanks constantly for whatever happens in your life; for the people you encounter, for each event in your life whether you think they are good or bad; for what you have and what you do not have; for what has been given to you and what has yet to be given. The most important thing is to be thankful every day for what you wish, as if it already came true.

3. Silence: Keep your dreams and goals to yourself, so you may accumulate within yourself as much energy as possible in order to materialize your dreams faster. If you tell anybody about your wishes, make sure you know what is in their hearts, as well as their thoughts and feelings toward you; negative words or energies towards you will slow down and make the materialization of your dreams harder."

After these words, Mr. Deeb got up from his chair indicating in a simple and polite manner that our meeting was over.

– "Until next week, son, and God bless you." He said.

– "Until then, and thank you for your time." I answered. I left the place with my heart swelling with happiness; I had so much information I was sure I would need more than this life in order to put it into practice, but what made me even happier was the thought of knowing we would get together again so soon. "What is a week when compared to eternity?" I thought to myself.

PART THREE

"We are unlimited beings, limited only by our
ignorance; no one is incapable, just
not trained well."

Mr. Deeb.

ABOUT THE RAW MATERIAL FOR OUR CREATIONS

The week went by pretty fast, making me feel like time was moving at warp speed. I was determined to enjoy the present moment, and remembering the many lessons learned the previous week, I set out to put them into practice.

I made my treasure map, and I very much enjoyed cutting and pasting on the board the images that represented all of my dreams; I was very proud of myself by the time I finished it. I felt happy as a child, like in that stage of our lives when we are able to dream big and without limitations of time or money. Too bad we castrate these feelings as we grow up and put limits to our dreams according to how much money we make. And what is worse, that we grow up to call such deplorable state 'being realistic,' because we ignore the fact that the most interesting thing in life is to have the capacity to increase our level of income to suit the size of our dreams so they may come true.

I began my objectives board with a cycle of decrees. I visualized myself completing each one of my objectives, paying close attention to every little detail, like an artist sculpting his masterpiece. I constantly invoked the light, and the feeling that I was doing the right thing permeated my whole being throughout the whole week. I felt more confident than ever about the future, with a deep sense of self-assurance that sprang from the deepest part of my soul and reminded me the words of a writer: *The world is yours, but you have to earn it.*

The certainty that anything was possible was born within me, and my inner limitations began to crumble away. I began to perceive, without a doubt, that I was moving from a stage of ignorance disguised as humbleness, to a state of pride that made my ego overflow. However, I was willing not to judge myself, and I told myself that maybe this was a normal process that anybody who begins to come into his or her own power has to go through.

I remembered a conference I once heard about false humility, or how we mistake poverty and mediocrity for humbleness. The speaker told us that humility is actually the step that follows pride. What this means is that as we are ignorant of our own potentials we manifest a false sense of humility because of our lack of self-esteem. However, once we discover our unlimited power and realize we can materialize anything we want, we tend to become full or pride and may even make the mistake of showing contempt for those who do not have the information that we have. He also reassured us that life itself makes sure that we transcend our ignorance through hardship and struggle, random events or coincidences; and that enlightenment would come when we finally recognize that all beings are equal. At the individual level, it is a process of letting go of the machine-like being or almost-animal state, and waking up to remember we were created in the image of God and that we co-create with Him. It is best to be wise, rich, healthy, loved and enjoy many blessings while at the same time remaining humble, rather than to aspire to be humble because of our precariousness. He also said that only someone who has actually been prosper and consciously gave it up has the right to say 'better humble and poor than proud and rich,' and not someone whose ignorance keeps him living in a continuous state of lack and presuming this is better than to be prosper.

I arrived thirty minutes early to my appointment with Mr. Deeb because I really wanted to continue to learn about the road of success. I wore my best suit; I wanted to make an impression on him and for him to see that I was turning into a successful person. I wanted his approval and for him to be proud of me. When I went into his office, his smile and the light that emanated from him struck me. I timidly and respectfully said 'hello.' He invited me to sit down.

– "How was your week?" He asked.
– "Excellent, Mr. Deeb." I replied.

– "Do you have any questions at all? Anything you wish to understand?"

– "Yes," I said, "I want to know if in order to be successful one needs to engage all the techniques you gave me last week at once."

– "No, use the one you prefer and mixed them up as you wish; for example, you may decree as you visualize."

– "I felt a little overwhelmed thinking I had to engage them all simultaneously." I confessed.

– "I understand, and I believe you will need a lot of time in order to put into practice what you will be learning. Did you do your homework? Living like a warrior of light, separating the light from the darkness and listening to your Christ within? Also, did you get to ponder about what is next in importance in the road of success?" He asked.

He left me dumbfounded, too many questions at once; however, I did not show it, though I suspected his intuition knew it all. I did my best to pretend I was not confused and proceeded to answer his questions.

– "I did my best to invoke the light at the beginning of a task and requested assistance from my Christ within in order to discern correctly between the information and my actions. I must confess that I forgot to do it many times. I did things without invoking the light or my Christ within and I only realized it after finishing what I was doing. However, I had never felt such union with God, I felt powerful, filled with energy; I remembered the following words from the Bible: "In can do all things through Christ who strengthens me," and I thought to myself that I was doing the right thing. I felt sad to think so many people are lost and disconnected from the spiritual."

– "You must be careful not to fall prey to spiritual pride and arrogance, which is to think you are in the right and all others are in the wrong, or feeling like you hold the ultimate truth. Simply recognize that you are in a certain part of your own road and others are in some part of theirs; everybody is learning, growing and changing, with the sole intention of – consciously or unconsciously – going back to Father, Creator, and to consciously live in Him forever. You must not think some people are going to be saved while others are in the wrong. The truth is not one soul will be lost; we only have the free will to determine the time of our trip back home and the experiences we will live in the meanwhile. Let your example, and not your words, be the source of inspiration for humanity. Now, tell me how it went with the road of success."

– "I dedicated some time to the task of pondering about what comes next in the road to success," I replied, "invoking the light, working with my Christ, and it occurs to me that the next step must be to control or select what comes through our senses." There was a long silence and I felt confident; I knew my response was correct, but I waited for him to confirm it.

– "Excellent," said Mr. Deeb, "you are now at the awakening stage, which consists on realizing things; each day you will observe to what degree it becomes increasingly enjoyable the experience of living in the light. The understanding that you cannot become separate from God and that by His side everything is possible will fill you with greater confidence. The first thing a successful person must do is to clearly establish what he wants – who does not know what he wants, has already arrived – and then become responsible for what he perceives through his five senses. To establish correctly what one wants is the art of thinking and creating our future. To control what we perceive through our five senses is the art of choosing how we feel; it is the raw material that creates our feelings. When we select the information, you are selecting your feelings. Our feelings are conditioned by previous experiences or information. Many people forget to experience new things in life and become trapped in the past; this is very dangerous.

A more elevated state of consciousness is to breathe deeply at each moment, which will instantaneously bring you to the present moment, and when you are in the present, your feelings do not arise from memory, but from your direct communication with God. When you adopt an open and receptive attitude in the here and now, you become capable of listening to your body telling you what to choose for your greater good; some call this a 'foretelling.' A lot of people think that to think is to feel, but I invite you to pay more attention to what your body is saying because it really originates from a higher level of wisdom and it never lies. Your feelings are sacred, they are expressed in the continuum of the present moment; your thoughts are usually conditioned by your past or the anxiety of the future.

In order to understand the importance of choosing the right kind of information to feed to your senses and the successful result that you desire, let us use the analogy of baking a chocolate cake. In order to cook this cake you need to put the flour in a bowl, add the butter, potatoes, coffee, sugar, raisins, shredded meat, mix it all together, place the container in the oven at the right temperature and then ask God – because you are a man of faith – to help you get an exquisite chocolate cake out of the oven. What do you think you will be getting?"

– "Regardless of my faith, whatever comes out of the oven will be disgusting, nobody will dare to try it. How can we get a chocolate cake when we did not even add chocolate to it?" I asked.

– "That is how it is," He answered, "what seems so ridicule to you is what the majority of people do out of ignorance, and even worse, they dare blame God for the results of their creations; they blame Him for what they obtain throughout their lives. It will be the same if you recorded a CD with Latin American music but in the end you were expecting to listen to classical music; no matter how much you pray, what you will hear when you play that CD will be Latin American music."

– "How do I apply these analogies to the road of success?" I asked.

– "Once you determine exactly what you want, you must fill your five senses with information that will help you fulfill your dreams," He explained. "For example, if what you desire is prosperity, it would be absurd to listen to the kind of news where everything they talk about is poverty or read about failing businesses, unemployment figures, people going broke or world poverty. That would be the wrong kind of raw material, such as pouring coffee to the cake batter expecting the cake to taste like chocolate."

– "That sounds like living in a fantasy world and forgetting about the reality we live every day." I said.

– "You either choose to be right or you focus on the results; successful people only focus on the results. What is the difference between reality and fiction? Most things that are possible today were impossible yesterday. In the art of creation, there are two kinds of people: the ones that wish to perpetuate their belongings or beliefs, searching for a way to see the future on what they do but sooner or later realize that both their belongings and beliefs became obsolete; until then, they will continually seek to perpetuate their past. The second kind are those who travel to the future with their minds and do not look forward to being right; on the contrary, they are willing to change their beliefs in order to create better and easier ways to obtain results; in this, they constantly bring their future creations to the present moment.

It is your choice to use your mind to remember history as it was made by others, or to create a new story, one made by you. What is important is to learn to differentiate between creativity and illusion, though they seem to be twins; creative people use action, while those who create illusions do not. Both come from the world of possibilities with the same opportunities to materialize their ideas, but inaction turns our dreams into fantasies. To perpetuate the past instead of creating a new possible future is a custom very much embedded in the way of being of the mediocre, those who sort of believe. What you capture through your five senses turns into the raw material that creates your thoughts, and your thoughts create the reality of your world."

– "How would I do, if I wish to help the poor, to not fill my whole senses with the raw material of poverty?" I asked.

– "Remember, you must live in this world but not be of it, and the best way to help the poor is by not being one of them, for those who have nothing have nothing to give. You must first fill your chests and then you can give love and abundance to everyone else. The five senses record this way: Your eyesight is constantly taking pictures of everything you see, it does not discriminate. It is an automatic camera that records absolutely everything. If you look at accidents, sickness, problems, sadness, poverty, loneliness, that is what you will record; the same is true if you look at prosperity, health, happiness and love. Some of the people who have studied the human mind have established that, on average, we record about 60,000 thoughts a day, more or less one per second. Concerning the images we observe, we record on average three times more, which means the majority of them are unconscious. Your mission is to focus on seeing more of what you wish to manifest in your life."

– "Then, if I see someone getting on an accident or a sick or poor person, should I ignore them and not help them?" I asked, and even though it was a spontaneous question, I felt that not to pause before speaking may have seemed rude to Mr. Deeb.

– "If it is in your hands to help, do it; otherwise is best to not get involved, you may in turn become a part of the problem. Most of the times, onlookers create massive traffic jams when driving past an accident just because they have to try to figure out what is happening on the other side of the road. However, they do not intend to help in any way and what is worse is they ignore that by putting their attention on the accident they create in their minds the need to have accidents in their own reality; and in some cases, they end up getting in the way of the real solution they are waiting in order to solve their problems.

Everything you see around you is "recorded" without analyzing whether it is true or not, and in the end it will turn into something certain whether you record from a magazine, a soap opera, comedy, movie, news program, newspaper or a billboard. This is the reason most companies spend so much money on publicity; you watch their commercial so many times that in the end you will feel the need to acquire such product or service. And repeat this, 'where I put my attention is the direction where I go.' Do it until it turns into an unconscious belief, and that will make you a more responsible individual."

– "So the mind does not know what is true or false?" I asked him. "My intuition tells me that we are much more than that, and we truly know what is true or not in the deepest part of our being."

– "No," he said, "our mind always records. Remember, for example, how you suffered watching the end of a movie that did not go as you wanted it, even though you knew it was just a movie, the fruit of someone else's imagination. For example, couples who wish to have a faithful, happy home, but always watch movies about infidelity and hate, cannot understand why they feel – unconsciously – attracted to those same kinds of behaviors."

– "Does that mean I should not watch television, go to movies, read the newspapers or magazines, and I should set myself apart from the reality of the world?" I asked Mr. Deeb. All of this information, along with my need to be right in front of him and the thought that maybe he was just testing my ability to use my own discernment, made me ask questions in a reactive way, seemingly out of line. However, I remembered that upon previous instruction he had warned me that those who react lose; and by reacting, they show little to no difference between them and animals, given the fact animals do not think but only react to a stimulus. In the end, I continued questioning the information: "Then, a doctor would not be able to see the sick, the lawyer would not see the one behind bars, nor could one go and visit the poor?"

– "The doctor's intention is to heal, and he is looking for a solution, not intending to be a part of the problem." Said Mr. Deeb. "The lawyer wants to free his defendant by looking for a solution, not a problem. If you focus on solutions, you will find them. Besides, you must become wise in order to choose what to put your attention on. There are inspirational movies, TV shows that give you valuable information without the morbid content you find in the regular news, books that inspire you. As you do this, what begins to happen is that you become increasingly selective, meaning, you make better choices about the kind of information you receive and become responsible for what you give your attention to."

– "And what happens with the other senses?" I asked.

– "The same;" He added, "whatever you listen to when you are asleep or awake, consciously or unconsciously, turns into the raw material for your creations."

– "So I will not be able to listen to the news on the radio or my favorite artists' songs?" I refuted, unwilling to accept this information I could not understand even though it sounded quite logic.

– "You can do anything, is just that you become more selective, as I said before, and the truth is that as time goes by you will feel the need to watch and listen to a different kind of information; you will enjoy different kinds of music and the conversations and people you associate with will be different as well. As you gather new information, you will create a new movie and the reality of your world will change as well. You may even move to a new house, have new friends, job... in short, if what you are recording is better, your results will get better as well. Have you ever heard about couples that go their separate ways after either one participated in a self-growth workshop, or after getting in contact with some new kind of information?"

– "Yes, many times I have heard about self-improvement workshops that ended up driving a wedge between couples. Why does that happen?"

– "It is not the workshop that does it, it is the programming they are receiving for their growth, being conditioned by the regent thoughts. The thoughts about God, the spiritual, our beliefs in the eternal, it all turns into our regent thoughts. Even further, when you do something that contravenes those new thoughts, you generate an automatic process of self-punishment or self-sabotage. Very quickly here, we will be studying this concept in more depth. However, for now understand that all sickness, poverty, loneliness, or any other negative state, is just a self-punishment mechanism, which is why it is so important to learn to feel innocent and unimpeachable. Of course, in a couple, when either one of them begins to grow in the direction of self-evolution and the other does not, what will happen is that in the future their programs will be so different that they will end up choosing to go in different directions. They will go away from what is known as the seventh dominant of attraction, the frequency within which a couple must vibrate in order to continue to feel attracted to one another. This is why it is so important for the couple to walk hand in hand in their personal evolution."

– "I know some happy couples in which one of them is not interested in any kind of self-growth activities while the other is, however, they continue to stay together. So, there appears to be some incoherence in what you are just saying." I said, and as soon as I finished my statement, I realized that once again I had expressed a very strong and judgmental opinion. He did not seem bothered by it though, because he never appeared bent out of shape or angry.

– "You continue to react through your judgments, which in turn lead you to disqualify my information all at once. It is wiser to ask for clarification in order to understand the other person's point of view." He replied. "In some couples, one of the two does not need to learn these self-improvement concepts because he or she already knows them, according to his/her evolution. What the other person does is come to the same level as the other in order to feel more fulfilled with the self and the couple.

Learn this about the art of human compatibility: at the physical level, we usually like what is opposite to us: robust people like thin people, tall people like short ones, and so on. At the mental level we also look for the opposite; if you are too analytical you will attract someone more sensitive. When you share with someone equal to you at the mental level, you continually compete with each other; as a result, you have greater conflicts with this person. You do not need to study the same as the other in order to share with someone else. Spiritually though, we do look for someone similar to us, someone who can walk hand in hand with us on the same path, someone at our same level of evolution. If you are honest, loyal and integral, you will be happy with someone who possesses all those qualities or values as well. Information gets you closer or farther away from certain people; always ask yourself what and to who are you making yourself attractive to or not. Again, it is important to be conscious and to choose what you listen to."

– "For me," I said. "it would be ok if I just stopped watching the news or chose which ones to listen to, but what about my favorite music artists? Their songs speak about suffering, melancholy, loneliness, sadness; almost always they turn to hits and top the charts."

– "There is what is known as critical mass, and that is what attracts you to what prevails on the planet. For now, this planet is basically negative: the news, movies, soap operas, news papers, jokes, songs, everything is negative and people like it; so, what is needed is more of us manifesting ourselves in the light in order to change the energy of the planet as a whole. As times goes by, more and more positive information will become available. Choose to listen to songs that inspire you, or listen to self-growth audio media that teaches you about the principles of success, and make sure that when you finish listening to it you feel energized, enthusiastic and ready to conquer the world. When you get that feeling inside of you, it means that what you have listened to has been processed through all five senses and it supports the achievement of your goals."

– "Does that mean my life is going to improve and many things will change just because I choose the information I receive?" I asked.

– "More than you can ever imagine." Said Mr. Deeb. "If you put into practice what you are learning now, five years from now it will be hard for you to believe you could have had the reality of the world you are having today, because it takes five years for your reality to turn into the equivalent of what you are reading and the people you associate with now. I want to talk to you about association: the environment that surrounds you conditions your behavior more than you can consciously determine; the prevailing emotions and thoughts in the air stick to you creating a need for it.

Very often, you find yourself reacting in ways you cannot understand, like as if you get out of control; sure thing is that in those moments you are being controlled by the energetic charges lingering in the environment. Always be vigilant, using your true sense of feeling to make sure you are in the right place; do not underestimate the energetic influence of the places you visit because they have a memory, and whether you are conscious of it or not, that memory latches on to you. If you constantly go to places filled with poverty, you will begin to attract poverty into your life; same thing if you go to a place where there is much violence, anger, violence, sickness, lust; but the same also applies if you go to places where prosperity, happiness, love and health abide."

– "Most people lack this kind of information, which is the reason so many homes have little awareness of the influence these external energies have on them." I added.

– "Unfortunately that is true." Said Mr. Deeb. "Many families wallow in the energy of lack because they talk excessively about poverty, which in the end leads to more lack; or they live in violence because of constant fighting without realizing that in time, and seemingly without rhyme or reason, they always find a way to be aggressive toward each other. It would be an excellent idea to watch all the thoughts and emotions we record in our homes because they remain in the environment."

– "What can a person do if, while giving a service to others, that person ends up going to a place of low vibration? Is the person harming himself by trying to help others?" I asked him.

– "When giving a loving service to other, the love energy around you creates a protective layer that prevents any kind of negative energy from latching on to you. You must be sure you are giving a loving service and not that you are merely feeding your ego, otherwise you will not be protected; this is a natural law, and you will end up infused with the negative vibrations of the environment. If you listen closely to your heart, you will understand he always guides you by letting you know where is convenient for you to stay or leave. Pay heed to these signs because they are Divine wisdom guiding you in your life. When you go to a church, you feel peaceful; at a disco, you feel like dancing; at a restaurant, you feel like eating. The environment in which we are conditions us.

Get used to lighting candles in those places you wish to change the energy into the light; this is the way to improve the energy because fire transmutes. Whenever you go through an unbalancing experience, put your clothes in the laundry and wash them, for all your emotions and those of the environment get recorded in them and water also transmutes all of these energies. You can do the same with yourself; get used to getting a shower whenever you desire to change your energies; take advantage of the moment and imagine the water is infused with light and that light cleanses your energy fields, infusing them with perfection. To be completely clean you bathe in the ocean; besides salted water, ocean water contains all the minerals. To walk barefoot in nature will also release all negative energies. Fire and pure air also clean; bonfires, candles, to breathe in nature, inhaling and exhaling very deeply in order to get used to charging your cells with good news. Deep breathing reminds us that something good is about to come into our lives; practice it continuously, it is good for you."

– "In regards to our association with others, how do other people influence us?" I asked Mr. Deeb.

– "You constantly associate with others without ever been aware that you become a magnet to the same results the people you associate with obtain; so, it is better to make sure the people you share with are getting the results you desire or are moving in the same direction that you are. Observe and become consciously aware of how you feel after you share with someone else, or after you go to a church, watch a movie, read a book or drive by a specific place; if you feel empowered and happy, it means that is a good association, otherwise it would be best to try to avoid it. Create synergy in your life on a constant basis, which means you must make sure that one plus one equals more than two. If you feel empowered after you leave a certain place, lived a certain experience or shared with a specific person, it means that is a good association and it is convenient for you; you only honor yourself when your association creates synergy."

– "What happens if I do not feel well after having shared with a family member?"

– "We will call those mandatory associations; it is a part of your learning and what is most important is for you to have the capacity to elevate yourself so you do not create an affinity with that which you reject. You must become the observer, which is God's perspective, an observer; He does not criticize or judge, so just observe, accept and elevate yourself so none of your mandatory associations can affect your wellbeing and happiness." Said Mr. Deeb.

– "What happens with the rest of our senses, touch, smell and taste?" I wondered.

– "You record in your cells every time that you smell. Learn to breathe in deep when something you like happens so you will program your cells with what you like and become attractive to it. If you receive good news, breathe in; if you pass a test, encounter someone special or if you feel happy, breathe in; inhale deep all the good things that happen in your life. When someone gives you a present, instead of saying 'Oh, do not worry, you did not have to go through all the trouble,' 'Oh, now I am ashamed,' breathe in deep as you give thanks and tell yourself 'I deserve this and much more.' To say it to the person giving you the gift would be foolish, but thinking about it opens you up to deserving even greater and to the possibility of receiving more and better each passing day. What we receive is what God sends to us through people, and what we give is what God gives to others through us. We are all messengers of Divine prosperity.

Something similar happens with the sense of taste. Associate the good times with pleasing flavors, and exquisite smells with pleasure and happiness. Your mind –designed to avoid pain and increase pleasure in your life – will once more attract the sense of fulfillment when it tastes those flavors that have already been recorded in your brain.

With regards to the sense of touch, every day open your hands and be receptive so the best can happen to you. When something that is not to your liking happens, shake your hands and move them from front to back to indicate that you leave it in the past. If you are with people or in a place you do not like, protect yourself through visualizing that you are inside of a great sphere of light so that energy will not penetrate. When you are faced with negatives emotions and all you do is just sit there and do nothing, all that energy just ends up all over you."

– "I have noticed you used the expression 'become attractive to, or a magnet to' quite often, exactly what do you mean by that?"

– "You have become attractive to many things in your life, in reality, to everything that exists in your world to this day; hence, to pay attention to what you attract is a good way to understand the way you are programming yourself on a daily basis. There are people who become attractive to poverty, loneliness, deceit, sadness, sickness, while others become attractive to wealth, health, happiness and love. When you observe your results and to what you are becoming attractive, you will be able to determine what you are recording through your five senses. Change the information you receive through your senses for something more balanced and for sure you will become attractive to greater things and better experiences. Before you attract something into your life, you must first program it in your cells and in your mind, just as the farmer who tends to his crop before it can harvest it; the more diligent he is with the tending of his crop, the better and more abundant his harvest will be.

If you wish to change the fruits, change the roots; if you wish to change the roots, change the seeds. That old saying tells you the world you see is a direct consequence of the unseen, and if you desire to change the external you must change internally your thoughts, words and the information you receive if this is not taking you to the place you want to go. You can consciously choose to change the information you receive, and the way to do it is to dedicate a part of your time to imagining what you want as vividly as possible, involving your five senses as much as you can. Another very effective method to accomplish the same is by having conversations with your own self."

– "And what would these conversations be like?" I inquired.

– "The self-talk technique is very simple: make an audio recording with your own voice saying positive messages directed to you in particular. Then, you let them play wherever you are; even if you do not pay attention to the audio, and even if the volume is very low, they will turn into the raw material to enter your brain in order to help create a new reality of your world. If you wish to, you may also play some background music, and it is better if your voice sounds relaxed and paused, as if you were telling a secret to someone else. You may also ask the people who represent authority to you, or the ones you admire and respect, to record the audio for you as a favor; these people can be your parents, couple, siblings, another family member or a friend. You can record it in the first, second or third person, using different phrases or affirmations and involving different aspects of your life."

– "Could you please give me an example?"

– "First, make a list of the affirmations you wish to program yourself with, such as:

I ———————————————, love and accept myself just as I am.

I ———————————————, completely enjoy my relationship with my couple, I guide my children to fulfill the mission for which they have been created, every day and in every way I am better, better and better.

I am connected to the wealth of the universe; I am the happy owner of ——————, etc.

Note: You may add as many affirmations or decrees as you desire, keeping in mind they should be in the first person, as an affirmation and in present tense.

Then, you may repeat the same affirmations or decrees in the second, and then in the third person, like this:

You, *here goes your name*, completely enjoy your relationship with your couple, you guide your children to fulfill the mission for which they have been created, every day and in every way you are better, better and better.

You are connected to the wealth of the universe; you are the happy owner of ———, etc.

And in the third person it would say like this:

Your name here, completely enjoys his relationship with his couple, guides his children to fulfill the mission for which they have been created, every day and in every way he is better, better and better.

Your name here, is connected to the wealth of the universe; He is the happy owner of ————, etc.

When your list of affirmations in the first, second and third person is ready, record them as an audio file. Remember, if you wish to have some background music, use something that sounds pleasant and relaxing to your ears, like some classical masterpiece.

Finally, play the audio file at a low volume while you work, sleep or when you think is appropriate. Do not limit yourself on what you desire because one day you will realize those recordings you used to play repeatedly, at such a low volume, are now perfectly reflected in your future. The conclusion is very simple: If your environment does not give you the information that you need in order to fulfill your dreams, you can create it, and your five senses will receive it as correct and it will become a part of your reality."

The silence that followed made me understand our conversation had reached its end. The fact I knew we had yet to finish the road of success, that in fact we still had a lot more to cover on the subject, it all filled me with a great deal of satisfaction because I knew I would be able to obtain another appointment with Mr. Deeb very quickly. Mr. Deeb was a very busy person and hundreds of people waited in line to have an interview with him.

– "To know what you want," He continued, "and to control the information you feed to your senses marks the difference for all human beings." He finished the session with these last words, which he spoke as if he was thinking aloud. "Put into practice the information I have been giving to you, because only applied knowledge persists in the spirit. Son, may God bless you and have a wonderful weekend."

– "Thank you," I replied, "same to you as well." I shook his hand and left his office. Although he had a very busy schedule, the secretary gave me an appointment for the following week. I must confess I was very happy to have such a privilege because it made me feel very special, like I was the chosen one.

When I left the building I was running and breathing in deeply, and when I realized how valuable the information I had been given was, I yelled at the top of my lungs 'I deserve this and much more!' I did not care whether someone could hear or see me.

Protecting ourselves from the information we receive

Unlike the previous week, this one had gone by slowly, filled with obstacles and altercations; in short, nothing went right. It seemed as if the world was upside down and my results were exactly the contrary to what I was trying to create through my decrees, visualizations and other techniques. Therefore, I began to wonder if this whole thing was just a scam, a pretty tale told by someone needing to be heard. He gave me a very powerful argument: all information must be logical, be proven and finally it must pass the most important test, seeing if it works by leading us to the result we are looking for; the thing is that every time I remembered the words I would be overtaken by doubt.

I also experienced a level of rejection for what I considered fanaticism on my part. I did not question Mr. Deeb's teachings at all, and I knew that only what I would manage to prove would be considered valid; the rest of it would be just another theory, and for now it did not seem to work. I thought about forgetting the whole thing; stop going to the meetings and leave those stories behind as another experience in life. However, sometimes our wishes are far from what destiny has in store for us, and moments later the rebel in me thought I would not be able to leave this joke just like that, so I decided to go back and unmask Mr. Deeb. I thought about telling him that none of his stuff worked. My attitude this time was very different from that of the previous week; I knew the rebellious child in me had taken over control. When I went into his office, he said hello in a very loving way, with a big smile on his face that would challenge even the uneducated.

– "Good morning, my son, how was your week?" he asked me.

– "It couldn't have been worse." I answered promptly, attempting to blame him or at least make him feel that he deserved my complaint.

– "And, how do you feel about it?" He replied.

– "Awful," I said, "nothing works, the world seems upside down, and now that I am so diligent with your recommendations – decrees and visualizations – it seems all I am attracting is the complete opposite!"

– "That is good!" He said, "You are finally going through what is termed the *test of the conqueror*."

– "I do not see what good can come from what is happening to me. Could you please explain further, because apparently none of your techniques work?" I said, with a certain tone in my voice that made it clear to him I was disillusioned and dissatisfied with the whole thing.

– "When you start to become conscious that you co-create with God, and that you consciously choose what you desire, and then you begin to practice a certain technique in order to materialize your desire, such as the decrees, you must go through two stages which are the *beginner's luck* and the *test of the conqueror."* Mr. Deeb's response did not afford me as much a chance to interject or ask any further questions. I am quite sure this was not the first time an apprentice had asked him these questions, so I had no other choice but to wait and listen attentively to what he was saying. "Beginner's luck manifests almost as soon as you decide to create something. It presents itself as a series of coincidences in your life that help to solidify your sense of confidence and determine that you are indeed in the right path to conquer your dreams. The test of the conqueror measures your level of certainty. Don't you ever forget this word because it is magical, and before achieving anything, the universe must know your heart is filled with certainty. Certainty is the state in which there is no doubt, faith is made manifest and the happiness of knowing what you desire will come to you in its proper time and place is the highest level of trust in God there can be. When you live in certainty, every moment of your life is filled with happiness, knowing that beyond all appearances, your desire is manifesting and you can trust and thank God. When you live in certainty, you learn to give thanks for what happens to you and what does not, for what you have and what you do not have.

Doubting is forbidden during the stage of the test of the conqueror. Doubt dilutes the energy you use to materialize your dream or it may override or delay your request. This is the reason so many things appear to happen to you, with emphasis on the word *appear*, things that are the opposite of what you are asking for. If a sales executive begins a session of decrees wanting to increase his sales and his best client decides not to buy something from him, he will probably think the decrees are not working or that he may be doing something wrong. The truth is both his conclusions are wrong, this is just the test of the conqueror, and as such, his attitude should be one of complete certainty that something better is coming his way and he will surely receive a far more superior client than the one he considered the best. Very often, you will find a person who begins a cycle of decrees and almost immediately it seems as if money hides from him, and he may even experience some temporary episodes of lack, the complete opposite to his decree; so never forget, this is the test of the conqueror. Pass this test and money will come to you without limits and in the most unexpected way.

If you begin to decree for your health, you may find yourself experiencing the exact same thing: you may come down with a sickness, or experience complications from an existing one. Just remember it is temporary, and the test of the conqueror only wishes to assess your levels of certainty in order to make you deserving of your wish. A common Asian motto says that nothing is permanent, all is impermanent and this moment too shall pass. Do not complicate yourself when you go through rough times, simply learn as much as you can from the experience because that lesson will too pass. Now, only the doers deserve to go through the test of the conqueror, life does not stop to teach the procrastinator. Until they commit to their own existence, life will not present them with the opportunities to let them know whether they are getting closer to or father from their objectives. Until the person takes definitive action, monotony will get the best of their lives. Some people think they are going through the test of the conqueror, when in reality the problem is they are dealing with the consequences of a continuous inability to take action and the lack of determination to conquer their dreams."

– "How can a person know if he or she is going through the real test of the conqueror?" I asked.

– "It is very simple:" he said. "If you are doing everything you can possibly manage, working as if your future depends on you alone and trusting that nothing happens if it isn't by the will of God, then only in those moments are you able to welcome the obstacles. Obstacles are the test of the conqueror disguised as problems; as soon as you overcome the test the price is yours.

On top of that, we are subject to the law of cause and effect during the *beginner's luck* and the *test of the conqueror* stages. What this means is that, many times, in order to achieve what we desire we must reap the fruits we have previously sowed. If in the past you spent a lot of time saying that your world was filled with poverty, then as soon as you begin to decree prosperity, and after a period of beginner's luck, you may in fact begin to reap the fruits of this previous crop. It may even be a part of your test of the conqueror, which is why it is so important to remain focused on what you want, so what you do not want may disappear from your life.

Another common mistake during the process of creation is to speak about it with people, especially when it is most unbalancing. First, get it into your head that when you complain about things, most of the people do not even care about what you are saying. Others are actually bothered by it, because they know you are dumping your trash on their reality with your complaints; and others are just plainly happy about your disgrace. Elevate yourself, be wise and do not talk about anything negative because on the one hand, you keep recreating it, meaning, you put the law of cause and effect into action and you will continue to attract into your life precisely what you are trying to get rid of. Allow your mouth to speak only words that represent what you desire to have in your life as a reality. Besides, you are only speaking about a part of the process; you have yet to possess all the necessary elements to make a proper judgment. It is just as if someone invites you to have soup at his place, and the moment you come into the kitchen and try what is in the pot, you realize that it tastes like water and salt. Then, you go ahead and conclude the entire meal is going to be horrendous without knowing your friend has just begun to prepare the soup and is in the first stage of its preparation.

Like the farmer in charge if his present, who sows and works as if it all depends on him but in his heart knows it really is in the hands of God - and it is all a part of heaven's grace so the perfect harvest will happen at the perfect moment,- to live in the position of the observer is to be in a very wise perspective because it is God's perspective. However, we prefer to live judging everything as good or bad, and the moment we do that we immediately anchor ourselves in those experiences. I invite you to learn to live in grace, in perfection, blessing what happens around you. For now, you do not have the conscious means to look at all of the processes of creation as a whole, so continue to think that you are walking hand in hand with God who knows all and acts in perfection. Know that He is having everything come together in perfect unison in order for your dreams, or something better, to come into your life."

– "Right now my tendency is to judge myself whenever I am out of money, as if I have to lie to myself by telling me that I do have it, or by trying to lie to others by pretending that I have money." I said to Mr. Deeb abruptly.

– "It is not about lying to yourself or others, it is about being wiser. You could choose to change some of your creations and give them a less permanent place in your vocabulary. Instead of saying "I have no money," you could say an affirmation like "I do not have the money right this moment." The difference is that with the first sentence you are creating something to be made manifest in your future, whereas the second sentence is merely stating what is at that very moment. You may begin to change phrases such as, "nobody understands me," for something like "at this moment, I have not made myself clear." You could also say, "up until now, I have only attracted people who do not understand my point of view." You can change, "I can't do anything right," for "Up until this moment, things have not come out as I wanted them to." "Nobody loves me," can be changed for "Up until now, I have not found the person who deserves to be my partner," "Up until this moment, I have only attracted people who reject me." You may change "I feel awful, I am sick," for an expression like "at this moment I feel sick, or I have pain in a certain part of my body;" "I never go out" can be changed for "Up until this moment, I have yet to go to a place I really want to go to."

Make sure your expressions state a specific time frame in order to avoid to continue creating or recreating what you do not want. Use wise words, such as *every day and in every way I am better, better and better.* When someone asks you "How are you doing today," or "How are you," you could answer in a very empowering manner, such as: progressing, happy, I am from better to greater, divinely, living in grace, wonderful, always better. You are an unlimited creator, so create the answers that will ensure a better and more empowering future for yourself.

ANTIVIRUS

In order to avoid being infected by information the does not support your creations, it is important to create an antivirus that will filter the information you receive; just as computers need it, so do you. The antivirus is a form of protection against the things that detour you from the road that leads to the achievement of your objectives. We have the capacity to choose the information we get through our five senses, however, we are not disconnected from what happens in our surrounding environment, and whether we understand it or not, we are more influenced by the thoughts, words and experiences in our environment than we like to imagine.

The antivirus works like this: You must become conscious of your five centers of power: what you visualize <the thoughts that remain in your mind>, what you decree <any word you say>, what you do and what you feel <divine feedback>. Everything you feel is sacred and is the way life shows you what is the right or wrong path, and it is also the food that gives you physical, mental and spiritual sustenance. Your physical nourishment is what you eat every day, creating, as a result, a healthy or a sick physical body. Your mental nourishment is the information you perceive either consciously or unconsciously through your five senses. Your spiritual nourishment is the prayer, talking to God; spiritual exercises, moving toward God; meditation, listening to God; and contemplation, seeing God in every living being.

How does the antivirus work? With the understanding that every word and thought creates your reality, when a thought or image of something you do not wish to manifest comes into your mind, just as when you consciously or unconsciously pronounce something you also do not want to materialize, you must immediately declare the following: *I cancel this for my persona*, or you can say *I erase this for my persona*. Choose an expression that clearly states that you are eliminating that creation using words like cancelled, I do not accept, erased, eliminate... either one of those works just fine.

With regards to your actions, when you discover that you have done to someone else what you do not desire for yourself, and being conscious that the law of cause and effect will bring to you what you do unto others, you should immediately stop performing the action you do not desire to see coming back to you, thus repairing in the moment the damage you may have caused.

As to your feelings, turn on your antivirus by listening closely to what your body says concerning a situation or person. Remember, you can determine when something or someone is not good for you: generally speaking, your body will feel pleased and filled with energy when you are surrounded by the right people or doing the right thing. In the same way, when you are doing something wrong or keeping bad company, your body will feel weak and you will experience feelings of discontent toward you and your environment. It is very important to associate correctly, and to know that associations that might have been good yesterday will not necessarily be good tomorrow. Listen to your body and follow its signs, this will prevent you from getting into trouble when you do not need to.

Have your antivirus <u>on</u> permanently; it will allow you to be conscious of what is going in through your five senses; in order to achieve this practice the prayer, asking for protection every morning, and remember that wherever you look at is where you are going. When you hear or see something that is not good for you, put it in the light so the hand of God may take charge of that situation or comment, and add an expression like: I do not accept it for myself o anybody else."

– "Does this mean the antivirus consists on consciously rejecting what we do not like by denying it out loud?" I asked Mr. Deeb.

– "Yes," said Mr. Deeb, "coupled with the intention of leaving everything, through the power of prayer, in the hands of God so perfection may manifest into your life. In the majority of the cases we are not even conscious of the information we receive, and it is through it that we receive so many viruses which penetrate through our five senses. Another very powerful antivirus that exists in the universe is to permanently love, serve and live in alignment with the Divine purpose."

This time, it all seemed more like a monologue rather than a dialogue, and what he was teaching me made so much sense and went so deep into my heart that for a moment I thought that every apprentice must experience the same sensation. As a result, the image of Christ teaching to his apostles came into my mind, and I envisioned them absorbing every word in a complete state of concentration and without a question. I felt sorry for myself, for having doubted Mr. Deeb, and just as if he could read my thoughts, he interrupted my silence:

– "Congratulations, you are now entering the path of light." He said.

– "What does one need in order to enter the path of light?" I asked.

– "You need to be a disciple."

– "And what are the characteristics of a disciple?" I continued.

– "A disciple is someone who is willing to let himself be guided to go on a path or to obtain a specific result. A true disciple displays these three characteristics: the first one is he is a good learner, open and receptive, willing to learn from his guide and knowing that the mind, like a parachute, only works when is open. The second one is discipline, which consists on doing what must be done at a precise moment. The difference between a disciple and a follower is that the former has internal discipline and does the right thing in the right moment, but the latter requires for another person to impose discipline on him and tell him what to do and when to do it. The third characteristic of a disciple, perhaps the most important and the reason I congratulate you, is discernment; in this, you have been a true disciple. Only when you are willing to question, and that question comes from a heartfelt need to understand something rather than our intellect or ego, is when you are a true disciple. Everything must go through a process:

information must sound logic, you must test it and then it must lead you to the place you want to go."

Although I remained silent, my mind was a in a whirlwind of thoughts. I perceived Mr. Deeb was assuming the position of the observer and chose not to judge how well I felt by having the privilege of being able to communicate with someone with whom I could see from that standpoint in life. I felt happy to know he valued my courage to question him, and that he knew my questions were real, coming from my heart and my desire to learn all that he was teaching me.

About the information

— "You must know that everything you receive through your five senses fills you up with information and knowledge." Added Mr. Deeb, this time as if time was a matter of importance running against us; I had the sensation he wanted to tell me many things without losing a single moment. He continued, "If you ask a random person about his profession, he will tell you that he learned it: A doctor goes to medical school; an engineer studies engineering; an architect studies architecture; a manager goes to management school and so on. No one is born instructed. The same thing happens with religion; most of the people learned it from their parents and grew up without questioning it; same thing happens with the language that you speak, so if you were born in Germany you would speak German, and if you were born in Italy you would speak Italian. The food you like depends on the place you grew up in, and you learned to feel more or less attracted to certain types of food. Your destiny would be different if you would have been born in another country, with a different language, religion, culture and paradigms, and all of it would certainly make of you a different kind of person.

From this, we can deduce the information and knowledge you posses came to you through your five senses, and as a result one can conclude several things:

1. Everything can be learned. If you wish to, you can become a great doctor, lawyer, engineer or

psychologist; you may practice whatever religion you desire, learn the language that you want and create an attraction for a certain type of food.

2. Limits do not exist, they are only self-imposed. You choose to set your own limits about what you wish to know, be, do or have.

3. There are no chosen ones. Each one of us chooses or rejects one's self. No one is incapable, just lacking the proper training.

4. You can change the information you have received if you discover new information that empowers you beyond the old one.

Be wise, remember information controls your destiny; improper information will lead to the wrong place or will keep you living a mediocre life. Always acquire new knowledge, such as knowledge on how to be happier, how to live more consciously and closely to God, how to have better health, how to have a more prosper life, how to make more and better friends, how to properly communicate, how to learn and apply principles of success. Acquire knowledge that makes you a better person, a better professional, a better student; and do not forget, there is always a better and easier way to do things. If you wish for a better future, choose correctly the kind of information so it may turn into the knowledge that leads you to your beliefs.

– "I can learn anything?" I asked, "So then, what about people's gifts, aptitudes and talents?"

– "In the universe where you and I live, everything is learned even though we do not remember when we actually learned it. You can turn into a person who possesses certain gifts, aptitudes and talents; all you need is to dedicate sometime of your day, every day, to the task of learning what you want. If you dedicate an hour a day to the practice of some form of artistic expression, in a year from now you would be an expert at the national level; five years from now you would be an expert at the international level." He said.

– "I am sure if I dedicated all of my time to singing, playing an instrument or painting, I would never get to be a great singer, musician or a famous painter." I said.

– "You are completely right about that," said Mr. Deeb, "not because you cannot achieve it, but because once you make such a strong declaration, by saying 'I am sure,' your creative power will manifest that reality. What I am about to tell you is just for you to let it linger in your mind and it will sprout as a certainty at the right time and place. Not all knowledge comes from this one life time, many of our talents have been learned in other lives; however, all forms of artistic expressions, unlike what we learn through our intellect, remain in our souls forever."

– "Does that mean there was a time neither one of us know of, when today's famous artists did not know how to properly sing, paint or act, and that it was through a learning process that they acquired those talents? Moreover, are you also saying that once a person acquires a talent, this talent will remain a part of that person's bank of knowledge forever? Meaning, one day in the future I will be able to be a talented genius of whatever field I choose?" I asked perplexed.

– "Yes, that's it." Answered Mr. Deeb, "And now that you have understood the points with regards to information and knowledge, I am going to introduce you to one of the most important subject on the road of success: beliefs.

About beliefs

Beliefs are learned, and this is the first thing you need to know about them. No belief is original; they are all the result of the information you receive through your five senses, so as you change the kind of information you receive, the beliefs will change as well. There are false beliefs, which are the ones that impose limits and take you away from what you desire; and there are true beliefs, which are those that empower and lead you to the fulfillment of your dreams or to the place you wish to go to."

— "In summary, what is a belief?" I asked, filled with curiosity and the ingenuity of a kid facing the unknown.

— "It is a thought of which you are completely certain; it is deeply embedded in your mind and it is simply unquestionable; it determines your limits and behavior with regards to what and how to do something in particular. When a belief is generalized, it is known as a paradigm or collective belief." Replied Mr. Deeb.

— "Does that mean one can develop new beliefs?"

— "Yes," he said, "and that flexibility is the key to evolution; many things that were thought to be true yesterday are known to be false nowadays. Let us first understand how beliefs are established: When you receive information for the first time, the most logic, immediate reaction is to deny it. However, as you continue to receive information, the arguments gain momentum and you become more certain, as a result, the doubt fades away and at that point the belief is complete. The two main problems to limit human creativity are doubt and fear, and the antidote or antivirus that you need are the following: you must fill yourself with information in order to combat doubt, and you must take action in order to combat fear. When doubt and fear disappear from your life, the results that you want manifest more quickly.

— "If I understood correctly, does that mean that in order to conquer our dreams we need to be certain? Or maybe it would be better to say we need to believe?" I asked Mr. Deeb.

— "You reach the belief through certainty, and this is the fruit of having the proper kind of information or when we consciously search and prove the information is right. It can also come from someone we personally regard as a figure of authority, and because of that, we do not feel the need to prove it right. The person can automatically install new beliefs in our minds. This is the reason I am so emphatic about the importance of practicing discernment on a continuous basis.

Let us take a look at these two examples:

1. When a friend comes to you with a new business proposal, the first thing to arise inside of you is doubt. Then, he presents you with the right kind of information and that gives you a level of certainty. Once you witness how many people enjoy being successful in that line of business, you develop the belief. So in the end certainty has been developed through information and the observation of the model being proved right.

2. When a person you regard as a figure of authority in the areas of religion, politics, science, economics or health goes public with a new paradigm, a new program or a new belief, and you choose to accept it as being true without a question.

Beyond the paradigms of good and bad, you need to learn to discern between a false belief and a true one, the difference being primordially this: all beliefs that prevent you from obtaining the results you desire are to be considered false, while all beliefs that lead you to the accomplishment of your dreams are to be considered true."

– "I am afraid to think the means justifies the end." I said frankly. "In other words, that I can do whatever I please as if it does not matter whether it is good or bad and everything is possible, that I can do and undo as I please. I think one must be careful; otherwise, one could end up trampling over others in our search for our individual dreams. We would give ourselves up to living a Machiavellian life style."

– "The antivirus for that belief is to continue to live always for the greater good, always making sure that your dreams do not come true at the expense of other and always determining the ecology of what you desire. Remember, the game of life can only be won when everyone involved wins. If someone needs to lose in order for you to win, or you need to lose in order for others to win, eventually you will all realize that you all have lost. Simply get busy with the business of not harming yourself or others, living in a constant state of 'I win- You win.'

Many of yesterday's unquestionable beliefs are known to be completely false today. Let us review some of them: 'The Earth is flat; those who are not baptized under the Catholic

Church will go to hell; women do not need education because they were born only to serve men; mankind cannot go to the moon; people of color are an inferior race; the atom cannot be divided; diseases like the leprosy, cancer or pertussis, cannot be cured; human beings are born with a pre-set destiny that cannot be changed.' No one agrees with any of those repulsive and obsolete ways of thinking anymore, thanks to human evolution and its rupture with old paradigms.

The process of bringing down many of the most popular paradigms gave birth to new heroes, new science geniuses, new leaders, new millionaires. These people, in short, gave birth to new ways of thinking and, with it, to a new world with a completely renewed quality of life. They invented the car; invented and improved the airplane; invented the way to travel to and conquer space; invented the desktop and the laptop; invented the phone and then later the cell phone; invented de Internet and communication via e-mail and chat; invented the cure for seemingly deadly diseases; recognized the value of women and their importance to society; opened up the minds of people to accept new ideologies and religions while respecting individual and collective beliefs, hence creating an environment of respect for all human beings.

These new creations re-invented the world and our way of living in it. You may not even imagine the changes that will come, but every day more and more people are willing to break with old paradigms and accomplish what seems impossible to others. You will surely witness teleportation, being able to travel from America to Asia in a matter of minutes; people who will choose to go spend their vacation in space or even those choosing to inhabit other planets. Do you realize many of those things you used to watch in science fiction movies have become a reality, all because of people who have broken old paradigms? Thank God, we continue to become more flexible in our capacity to change our beliefs, especially when we realize they do not work. Remember, your beliefs can either limit or empower you; been conscious of those that take you away from the results you desire and which bring you closer is taking a step toward excellence.

One could say that learning to think is not necessary. However, one of the main reasons human beings suffer so greatly is because they do not know how to think. To know what to think is to determine exactly what the person wants, beyond the limits of time, money and what people deem possible or impossible based on their beliefs. To know how to think properly is to focus your internal dialogues in order to determine the benefits – sometimes hidden – from obtaining the opposite results to what we want. To know how to think, son, is to dedicate fifteen or twenty minutes every day, when you wake up or before going to bed, to the task of finding all possible successful solutions to your problems. To do that is to know how to think."

Some limiting beliefs

- To feel guilty, rejected, ugly, a sinner, undesired, unworthy, not enough, incapable or unable... The antidote is to feel useful, innocent, unimpeachable, capable and dignified.

- To think destiny is already written, and we are victims of destiny... The antivirus is to feel we are one hundred percent the creators of our results, responsible for what we attract and what we project to the reality of our world.

- Nobody supports me; they envy me and always want to take advantage of me... The antidote is to believe in people and trust them, as well as their capacity if that is the case, until they show to the contrary.

If you look at the people who get the results that you want and you imitate their beliefs, no doubt you will obtain the same results as theirs. Let me tell you four of the most common beliefs every person of success has:

FUNDAMENTAL BELIEFS

1. Belief in God. They completely believe that the hand of God runs everything and they have an established form of communication with Him in which they believe. They do not need to belong to an organized form of religion in order to be successful; every religious person is successful: Catholics, Protestants, Jehovah's Witnesses, Buddhists, Shiites, Muslims, etc. The important thing is to believe completely in God and to have an excellent form of communication with Him, meaning, to have a continuous form of connection with the Source. They know they can attain everything with God by their side because he gives them strength.

2. They believe in themselves. They know they were created in God's image and He gave them the power to co-create with Him; limits do not exist and they are only self-imposed; there is no one on this planet who is more or less than they are because we were all created equally, yet with the ability to be unequal. They never sell themselves cheap, demanding the best from life and in return giving the best of them.

3. They believe in others. Never underestimating anybody, when they talk to someone they know they are in the presence of an unlimited being, limited only by his own ignorance; They do not see others for what they have but for the magic of what they can be, treating everybody with respect. They find communication as a form of art that allows them to treat others better, and are used to seeing God in the eyes of every person.

4. They believe in what they do. They love what they do and feel proud to do it; their work is not for the world bur for God because they see work as a means to give back to the world for all the blessings in their lives. They know that to serve and to give is part of the purpose and sense of life. They are very clear about the

> fact not one type of job is better than other, and every day they strive to do the best they can at what they do as a form to give thanks to the heavens. They prepare themselves every day in order to serve better and in the most appropriate way, knowing everything can be improved, and being weary of not falling in the hands of the syndrome of the finished product – believing they have arrived at perfection and there is nothing else to be improved – least mediocrity reign in their lives."

– "Just by holding those four beliefs my whole life could be turned around for the better?" I asked.

– "Surely," He replied. "And if your results do not improve is because you are not living up to one of these four fundamental beliefs."

– "How can I improve on my beliefs?"

– "Through information; read books that foster these four beliefs, listen to audio, watch movies, go to seminars, associate with people who are loyal to these beliefs. And one other recommendation: it is never enough." He added.

– "It is never enough?" I said. "Would not that be like spending your life in a state of constant dissatisfaction? I do not understand."

– "Your belief in God, in yourself, in people and what they do, that is never enough. You can always increase your levels of belief, and the more the better; read sacred books in order to increase your belief in God, practice prayer, meditation, contemplation and spiritual exercises. In order to augment your belief in yourself, read self-help books. The best ones are autobiographies. Listen to audio on self-improvement techniques; associate with the right kind of people; love yourself unconditionally; accept your past for good; forgive yourself for all the guilt you may have felt; feel worthy of the best, living always in first class and not selling yourself cheap. In order to increase your belief in people, always expect the best from them; constantly edifying them, focus on their qualities and avoid talking about the negative in people; do not let your judgments lead you to believe that what you think is true; when you have the opportunity to serve them, do it. Read books on how to properly relate to others, and in order to increase your belief in what you are doing, inform yourself on the most profound and technical aspects of your profession; find arguments that give your profession a higher sense of purpose. Ask universal guidance so what you do in life is connected to your purpose, and fill yourself with arguments for the betterment of your environment, to bring happiness to people thanks to what you do.

If you observe with the sensitivity of someone who wishes to learn at any given moment in life, you will be able to observe how beliefs change from one country to another; here then lies the difference between the results obtained. There are countries where people believe more in God and they have a better form of communication with Him, while in other countries it would seem as if it was the reign of Sodom and Gomorrah, hence, their results are chaotic. In some places, people believe more in and are proud of themselves, they focus on believing, discovering, investigating, and as such they always prosper and believe in what they do; these people search for and apply the concepts of total quality, are always innovating and making better what already exists. In other countries, people are used to copying other's works; it would seem as if they ran out of creativity and wallow in routine; nothing is original and poverty, sickness and violence are the order of the day. There are many other countries where people believe more in others and are more respectful of human rights, while in other countries people treat each other worse than they treat the animals.

Customs are very different as well. In some places, people are not allowed to create or think; in others, innovation is rewarded. Some countries have no regard for women, while others have women as their leader. Some religions teach through fear, others through love; in some places, they teach about self-punishment and self-flagellation; in others, it is forgiveness and acceptance.

Choose well your beliefs, son. You need much courage and discernment in order to be willing to question and change the beliefs that do not serve you any longer. Control the information you receive and you will control your beliefs. The more and the better the information, the more empowering your beliefs; the less information, the more dependent you are. You must pay attention to and recognize when someone is trying to program you; keep your antivirus on all the time. When someone tells you that you cannot do it, that you cannot achieve something; when someone sets any kind of limits on you, cancel it. And what is more important, if it is you or a close friend who is imposing the limits, a family member or a person you consider to be some sort of authority, that is when you need to be alert because the limitation could be automatically installed as a new form of limiting belief.

Become selective and maintain your capacity to discern one hundred percent of the time. Do it continuously so you become aware of the programs attempting to be installed in you through religion, your profession, friends, parents, partner, children, etc. Remember, even you install - consciously or unconsciously - new forms of belief in your own self through your internal dialogues, visualizations, decrees and affirmations. Learn to self-install empowering beliefs through advertisement."

– "How could I do an advertisement when I am not in the advertising industry?" I asked.

– "It is very simple." He answered. "Let us analyze what advertisements are good for. Advertisements allow you to learn about new products or services, making you believe they are of excellent quality and creating in you the need to have it.

Once you understand the purpose of the advertisement or commercial, you make it in such a way that it will cover your needs. You give it the emotional tone needed to make an impact and play it frequently enough for it to be remembered. In order to install empowering beliefs, your advertisement should fulfill the same pre-requisites:

- Last no more than thirty seconds.

- Use empowering words that reflect or connect you with the states of happiness, pleasure and fullness.
- Let it clearly express the results you wish to achieve or the kind of person you wish to be throughout the day.
- Read it when you get up in the morning, aloud, in front of the mirror; repeat this routine every hour until bedtime. You will notice a rush of energy and coincidences that lead you to the materialization of the reality of what you have written down.
- A new belief is installed in you and it will lead the results you obtain during the day.

Example of an advertisement to increase sales:

I, ——————, am the best —————— salesman. Today, I attract into my life people who enjoy shopping for my products at the price I sell them to. God opens my doors to those who need my products and the universe conspires for me to reach every one of them easily and pleasantly. I feel happy; the day's sales goal of —————— has been surpassed greatly.

Example of an advertisement to increase your friendships:

I, ——————————, love and accept myself just as I am. I attract into my life people who love and accept me just as I am. Every person I encounter has something important to offer so that I may fulfill the purpose for which I was created, and he or she provides me with a specific lesson for my future. Every day, I have more and more loyal, prosperous and integral friends. I am enthusiastic to see the amount of people I will encounter today.

Example of an advertisement to increase happiness:

I, ——————————, am better and better each and

> *every day and in all ways. Today is the best day, I deserve the best and I accept it right now. All is prosperity in my life. God guides me and He is with me now. I constantly manifest the purpose of my life from the light of my heart; in my world, everything is perfect and I am safe. Today, I feel happy and all human beings bring me good news.*

What is important is for you to take into consideration that creativity is infinite, and get used to creating your own advertisements according to your needs and judge them not by how well you made them, but for the results you obtain. These commercials work very well and fast; you do not need to wait long in order to see how well they work. In about nine days, you would have already noticed the difference in your results.

The three stages of creation are the following:

- First stage is denial, in which it appears as if your results are the complete opposite to what you are creating; these being the fruit, of course, of previous creations. It is like when you clean your house and you put all the trash from the rooms in the common hallway; if someone were to come over to your house right at that time, their judgments might lead them to think your house is very dirty, when in reality it has never been so clean. At this stage, you experience the test of the conqueror of which we have already spoken about. This step allows you to test the strength of your belief in the possibility of manifesting your desire, and it is exactly the stage at which most of the people give up their dreams because they cannot push themselves to go beyond the difficulties and learn to trust and wait.

- The second stage is about proof. This is the stage in which the evidence invites you to believe that what you are doing is right. You feel the energy is in your favor and experience the knowingness that everything will happen at the right place and time.

- The third stage is certainty; this happens when you harvest the fruits of what you have been creating; it is in your hands. Some people – out of ignorance – tend to look at this stage as merely having good luck, but if they take a close look at the circumstances, they will see they have only correctly applied the principles of success."

— "Does every creative methodology goes through these three stages, whether they are mental, advertisements, decrees, visualizations or something else?" I asked Mr. Deeb.

— "Yes," He said, "any method you choose in order to create will go through these three stages. As you master the art of creation, you will go through them more quickly." Then he added, "Son, our next meeting will be in fifteen days." He said as if he was telling me we would meet again in the afternoon. It was a very productive meeting and now it had come to its end. Even though Mr. Deeb did not need to tell me with words when he had decided to end the session, I immediately understood it though I tried to protest, 'why do I have to wait such a long time for our next meeting?' I asked myself. I did not have the guts to ask him because I knew the time he dedicated to me was way more than the time he gave to others, so that made me think I should in fact be more grateful...When I realized I was judging myself I decided to toss that thought. Through the window in his office, I could see a couple who seemed to have forgotten about the world around them because they were passionately kissing one another; I assumed they were saying good-bye to each other. I smiled at my own internal dialogues when I remembered something I once heard: One does not see the world as it is, but as one is. "You have a lot of information you need to evaluate and discern through, and what is more important, you need to put it into practice. I was happy to see you; I know this material will afford you a wonderful experience. God bless you."

— "Thank you," I said immediately, "I wish the same to you." I left the place determined to put all my ideas in order. I felt radiant, filled with light, however the weather was not the same for the sky was pretty dark even though it was just four in the afternoon; the sound of thunders spoke of an oncoming massive storm. I thought about the environmental complications as another test to the conqueror because I had to run several errands and I did not have a car, but nothing and no one would take my inner happiness away; though it was a very unusual kind of thinking, it felt nice to observe I was not judging myself for it.

Throughout the course of the following two weeks, all my reflections were designed to, more than question, learn and put into sequence all the steps on the road of success:

1. To know exactly what is desired; to be able to establish it through all five senses, putting it into the appropriate kind of context, the when, where, how and with who, as well as the proper ecology of the desire, thinking and conditioning for the greater good and the highest of ends.
2. To select the kind of information that comes through the five senses in order to make sure it leads to the conquest of what is desired.
3. To be vigilant, keeping the internal antivirus always on so that any time the wrong kind of information – the one that takes you away from what is desired – comes to either one of the senses, one is capable of denying it entry.
4. Fill one's senses with empowering information, recognizing that beliefs are certainties that can be altered consciously, and knowing some of these beliefs are true and others are false.

That is to discern, I thought, filled with pride at the thought of being right and feeling like I wanted to shout it from on top of a mountain. I wondered what would come next. For the course of those fifteen days, I did my best to create the habit of reading. I discovered that there is much literature on the four fundamental beliefs. It bothered me to know people hurt each other, and the thought of so much discord out of the mere need to be right, prompted me to make a promise to myself: "From now on, I will never desire to be right because this is the reason there are winners and losers; let someone else be right, I just want to obtain the results." Therefore, I was determined to make this my very own private motto and banner. Yes, for the fruits they shall be known. I did not want to be recognized in the world for my words, but for my example, and God was giving me the clues as to how to do it through Mr. Deeb.

Reading was not my forte, so I barely moved forward with my first pick: *Traveling light*, by the Jesuit priest Carlos Valles, in which he narrates his experiences while taking a course with his friend and spiritual guide, Mr. Anthony de Melo. For me, reading this book represented a real breaking with my old paradigms; thanks to Mr. Deeb's words on discipline, I forced myself to read one page per day, which was not much but at least I was being disciplined about it and that made me feel like a true disciple. I thought to myself that if I was not able to do it, I would be in need of someone else to teach me how to be disciplined, and then, I would be no more than a mere follower.

Many things happened, and even though I had new and good information, I was not always able to apply it. It seemed as if there were two different people inside of me entering into a conflict; on the one side I was reading the book on self-development, and on the other I could not miss the afternoon news on the TV, even though I knew all I was doing was filling myself with negative information. I would listen to inspirational audio on the principles of success, yet at the same time I would listen to music filled with unbalanced messages. Although I wanted to associate correctly and I would meet with friends in order to talk about empowering subjects, I also shared with some coworkers who are used to criticizing everyone and everything.

"How incoherent!" I thought to myself. I wondered what Mr. Deeb will say when he finds out I am not putting into practice his teachings one hundred percent of the time, even though every time we meet I demand that he give me better and more detailed information. What will be the use of everything I am learning if I am not putting it into practice? It was important for me to be able to tell Mr. Debb about all of these inner conflict I was experiencing; I promised myself I would be sincere with him on our next appointment, and I will let him know what was happening on my day to day. This would be my way of taking as much advantage as possible of this unique gift that life had put in my path: Being taught by such a special person. When I realized I was feeling so honest, I felt more deserving and worthy of these teachings.

PART FOUR

"Expect the best at every moment of your life and of the people you encounter, and so it will be."

When is too late to love

ABOUT OUR INTERNAL DIALOGUES

As it happens so often in life, the time for our wishes to be fulfilled always comes. I looked forward with much happiness and enthusiasm to my meetings with Mr. Deeb, always wishing for them to never end. However, I was forgetting two of the principles he taught me: "Nothing is permanent, everything is temporary" and "all things have their season, and in their times all things pass under heaven." *Ecclesistes 3*.

This week I needed to go deeper, learn more, take advantage of every second, and for that I needed my senses to be as sharp as possible; at the same time I felt riddled with fear, and my internal dialogues, rather than increasing my levels of happiness, helped only to add more wood to the fires of anxiety. "I should not make any kind of judgments," I thought to myself, after all, the master appears when the student is ready; everything is perfect, and what I need to learn will be recorded in me. However, I should bring a voice recorder to make sure I do not miss one word, not an ounce of all the wisdom this magnificent old man, who had chosen me as his disciple, had to share.

– "Welcome back, son, how did you do these past couple of weeks? Tell me; to what conclusions did you arrive?" Ask me Mr. Deeb.

– "Better with each passing day, although I felt very anxious." I said, feeling very proud of my answer. "I was analyzing your teachings, and even though I was able to keep the information present, many times I failed to put it into practice. Very often, the man I have been keeps putting himself over the man I desire to be. I wish to live a more prosperous kind of life, yet I continue to watch the news where they speak about the ever increasing levels of poverty in the country; I read novels where the heroes are very poor people and the rich are the evil ones; I watch horror movies that throw me into a state of panic, anguish and despair; I listen to music with lyrics that speak of limitations and I do not want to program myself with those because I do not want for those to be the results I obtain in life. In truth, I feel pretty much incoherent."

– "In spiritual terms, that is called *waking up*. In the beginning, you live in a state of unconscious ignorance; then, you move on to a state of conscious ignorance. After that, you become conscious of your information, and lastly, you live in a state of unconscious wisdom. All of these will happen a little at a time. Certainly, what really matters is what you tell yourself, your internal dialogues, what some call attitude. Be careful not to judge yourself, that can deteriorate your self-esteem and self-image, but we will talk more about it later. Celebrate that you are entering the third stage of knowledge. Observe yourself but never judge; you will find many who will volunteer to do it for you because they are just waiting for the right moment to judge you." he said with a smile on his face. And what a beautiful smile he had! I felt as if he smiled not with his face, but with his soul. He was so filled with light that I would have liked to have the chance to film the whole scene with a video camera, although this was not possible, but still, it remained forever imprinted in my memory.

"All human beings go through that kind of experience, where life, as soon as it gives us the possibility to learn something new, almost immediately gives us the experiences that will allow us to apply what we just learned. We do not always put it all into practice; in reality, what is common is that people continue to make the same mistakes. However, now you start to become aware of them. As time goes by, you change a little at a time and so does everything around you; your friends, your finances, your health, the way you enjoy things in life and much, much more. These changes will happen to you automatically, and the speed at which they happen is relative to each person's beliefs; for one person, changing may be a slow and painful process, while for someone else it may be quick and painless; limits in terms of time and degree of difficulty are self-imposed.

If you were to choose to change everything now, at a rhythm different from what your intuition dictates and without living your own process; if you were to be stubborn about transforming your life and chose everything you desire, the information and beliefs; after a while, there is a high probability you would end up rejecting the new results and would go back to the place from where you first started. Critical mass, or that which dominates your surroundings, will try to bring you back to the old over and over, to the old person you used to be.

If you do not live your lessons thoroughly, respecting the individual process and allowing yourself to be protected by your own discernment; if you just take things at face value, what you end up with is fanaticism and violence among human beings. Most of the people fight because they want to be right about the information they have. However, the idea is to take all of that information and turn it into an experience, then the arguments disappear, nothing is being judged because to talk from experience makes a big difference. Politics and religion are two of the most dividing subjects in life. The best thing you can do is to understand that people believe what they believe and they are convinced about it, but you already know you do not want to be right, you just want the results. When the critical mass – or the amount of people needed to activate a new paradigm – of people who think they are right is reached, and someone does something to the contrary, something that takes their beliefs out of context, the majority will try to trap this person and reel him back to the collective belief that dominates them. These people are honestly mistaken; a person can be honest, yet be honestly mistaken.

Forgiveness is a word that many people use; however, it will be hard to forgive others if you do not first forgive yourself for what you did wrong in the past, at least according to your own judgments. By the way, fables contain a lot of eternal wisdom in them; it is presented to children in a format that is easy to comprehend, while adults find it more difficult because they tend to rationalize everything, and it is that rational mind which gets in the way of going deeper in knowledge. Jesus spoke in parables in order to be able to deliver knowledge; children's stories are a way to deliver a lot of information. Let us analyze, for example, Aladdin's tale: in this tale there was Aladdin, the cave, a lamp, a genie, a carpet and three wishes. Aladdin is each one of us; the cave is our physical body; the lamp is our heart; the genie is the divine spark, the part of God that lives within our heart; the three wishes refer to the spiritual, mental and physical desires; rubbing the lamp is the equivalent to activating the Christ energy within, which is accomplished by means of forgiving ourselves, forgiving others and requesting others' forgiveness; and the peace that is experienced by flying on the carpet as it takes Aladdin to where he wants to go, is inviting us to have the right kind of feelings we need in order to manifest our desires, such as feelings of faith, certainty, trust, and the most important: complete forgiveness for the damage we have done unto ourselves in thought, word, deed or by omission, whether we remember it or not. We must also ask for forgiveness from those we hurt and send our forgiveness to those who hurts us at all these levels. This is how miracles happen; this shows the importance of forgiveness in order to unleash our unlimited potential. When we consciously activate our Christ energy, we are consciously eliminating our limitations. A higher state of consciousness will invite you to change the need to forgive yourself or others, for the need to give thanks to you and others for the experiences you have lived; because of those experiences you are the person you are today. People go through life regretting and resenting others, ignoring this is the main reason for their state of lack. Additionally, they also create so-called terminal illnesses as a form of self-punishment."

Having finished his sentence, the office became unusually silent, making me think his contemplations went deeper than any word could ever describe. The atmosphere seemed suddenly overtaken by a kind of sadness and nostalgia. However, I knew from experience that Mr. Deeb had the ability to change any feeling or emotion in the blink on an eye.

– "Let us talk about our next step on the road of success." He said calmly, so much so that I could have thought whatever I had just felt was just a figment of my imagination, a misperception that had never existed.

– "Which one is it?" I asked rapidly, in an attempt to avoid thinking I was being rude in trying to analyze my guide, my master teacher.

– "Attitude." He said. His answer was short and dry.

'That is a good way to prevent my inner narrator from robbing me of my energies.' I thought to myself.

ATTITUDE

"The way you think when you lose determines how long it will be until you win."

David J. Schwartz

"Attitude is the way you react to experiences or situations in life; it is conditioned by what you say to yourself at every moment of your life – this is determined by your inner dialogues - and it controls eighty five percent of your results, while your aptitude controls fifteen percent. And if I remember well, most of the information given to you at universities is aimed at improving your aptitude, which undoubtedly is the reason so many people to fail as a professional. This is the reason why learning to straighten your attitudes as quickly as possible is so important, remembering to focus only on the results.

For those of us who live in grace, the ratio of eighty five to fifteen percent is different. We know that attitude is everything and it determines one hundred percent of our results. Attitude, or our internal dialogues, which is the same, is what prompt us into action or freezes us into place. Because of this, what we say to us or the information we receive are of utmost importance, for they can direct us immediately into action. Both, our inner dialogues and the information we receive, have the power to paralyze us and give us a sort of mental obesity; we have the solution to all our problems but nothing happens in our lives.

Now, going back a couple of steps on the road of success: If you desire to change your attitude you must change your beliefs; in order to change your beliefs you need to change the information that you have; in order to change the information you need to select what enters through your five senses; and in order for all of this to be coherent, the most important thing is to know exactly what you want. The best attitude is created when you think, talk, feel and act as if what you desire has already materialized in your life."

– "I continue to think this is a way to fool ourselves and take us farther away from the reality of our world." I said, interrupting his lecture in a very abrupt manner that simply bordered on criticism.

– "It would only be self-deceit if you were trying to convince yourself or if you are trying to convince someone else of something false; if you presume and give a false impression in front of others. What I am saying to you is to stay open, in receiving mode, that way you will achieve faster whatever it is you are trying to manifest; this attitude is something you do with yourself, not with the external world. You convince yourself that what you desire has already become a reality; this is the highest level of faith, which is called certainty. Remember: Faith in the future means strength in the present. Besides the four fundamental beliefs (believe in God, in yourself, in others and in what you do), there are other beliefs to help empower your attitude:

- Everything that happens is for your own good. You can always learn a thing or two from every experience.

- To worry about things is to doubt God who is in charge. Do not be pre-occupied, be occupied; preoccupation is earning interests in a debt you do not have. Ninety five percent of things you worry about never happen, they are nothing more than a monster created by your imagination.
- Your internal dialogues can turn hell into paradise or vice versa.

- Nothing is permanent, everything is transitory; even the happiest and most difficult times will too pass. Everything we have is borrowed from God, all material things, our families, everything. Instead of saying "my house, my car, my clothes, my farm, my parents, my wife, my children, etc." it is better to realize that using the word "my" is self-deceiving; everything is a loan from God, so enjoy it without attachments and learn to live every single moment of your life to its fullest.

- When faced with a seemingly insurmountable obstacle, repeat the following to yourself: I can do this, it is very easy and I will achieve it.

- The best way to have the proper attitude is by formulating the proper questions.

- Proper physical posture will greatly improve your attitude; like keeping your back straight, for example.

- To focus on the problems creates more problems. It is only when you focus on the solutions that the wisest part of you can give you the right answer. Focus on the right solutions, keeping an open and receptive attitude to the signs from the universe.

- Enjoy every second of your life as if it was the only one; the right question to ask yourself would be, "what must I do here and now in order to increase happiness in my life?" Whatever the answer is, do it; just make sure you do it for the greater good and the highest of ends.

- Recognize that life is worth living when the following premises are met: if you learn; if you enjoy; if you serve. Make sure, at every second of your life, that you are fulfilling at least one of these, and even better if all three are being fulfilled at the same time.

- The following are key characteristics particular to a successful person: they focus on results while the rest of the people focus on the process. Successful people talk about the future and focus on living fully in the now. The present is a gift God gives you on a moment-to-moment basis; those who fail live their lives wasting the present by living in the past. Successful people talk first about the past and then about the future, speaking more about the future than the past. Successful people learn fast from their negative experiences and focus on the positive. In short, you first talk about the process and the past, and then you focus all your attention on the positive, the successful results and the future.

I will give you a list of things that will help you sustain the right kind of attitude, and you should revisit it every day like a pilot does with his check list before takeoff.

- Begin your day with a prayer that comes from your heart, stating God is your partner and journey companion.

- Bless your food and leave every new experience and the day's events on God's hands.

- When you take a shower, feel how besides water and soap, there is a light bathing your body with the ability to cleanse and protect your environment.

- Wear the best clothes you have today, because saving them for a special day is to assume today will not be special. Wear them with the expectation that today will be the best day of your life. Most people do not realize the way they prepare to begin their day determines, in great measure, its results.

- Always feel you deserve the best: live in first class and do not sell yourself cheap; life will give you exactly what you choose.

- Copy the people who get the results you desire.

- Make sure when you look at something or someone, that it is only acceptance, sweetness and, most importantly, light which emanates from you because your eyes are the mirror of your soul. Even if you have not opened your mouth yet, your gaze can project aggressiveness or tenderness, acceptance of rejection, patience or impatience.

- When you speak to a person, look at the person's left eye. This will tell the person's unconscious mind that what you are speaking has authority and credibility. Additionally, to look into their eyes as you speak is a powerful tool to increase your self-esteem and self-image.

- In your mind, let the God in you say 'hello' to the God in the person you speak with. To do this will make the other feel respected, loved and recognized.

- Your handshake speaks volumes about your attitude at the moment you first say 'Hi' to another person; a weak handshake denotes a weak character, while too strong of a handshake denotes an insecure and aggressive person. Because of this, when you first greet someone, be secure of yourself when you shake their hand in order to let them know you are important, but not so strong to where they will consider you aggressive.

- Get used to calling people by their proper name; leave the name calling for the ignorant. When you first meet someone, take whatever time you need in order to learn and remember their name; for anybody, being called by their own name is one of the sweetest things they can ever hear. When you are called by your own name, the message your unconscious mind receives is that you are important.

- Smile; a smiling person reflects happiness and the unconscious message is that this person is the bearer of good news. At the beginning, you will feel you are only smiling with your face, but then you will smile with your heart. Following, you will feel as if your smile is coming from your soul, celebrating the mere fact of being alive. Unless you have a very strong reason not to, please, smile.

- Walk fast; this sends the message to others that you know where you are going. The most precious thing people have is their time, and every successful person makes sure every minute of their time counts. Except some special circumstance calls for doing otherwise, walk faster than the average people around you.

- Never be late for an appointment. Get used to arriving five minutes earlier, for when you arrive late you are disrespecting other people's time.

- When you go to a meeting or event, sit in the first row or as close as possible to the stage. These seats are usually reserved for the VIPs, and as soon as you choose to, you will become one of them. Acting as if your wishes have already come true, living as if, thinking as if, talking as if; it will all help you achieve what you desire quicker.

- Speaking with force and louder than others is also a sign of self-confidence and a proper sense of self-image. Do not interrupt the other person when he speaks; be an active listener and take notes if it is something important, nodding your head as a way to show your approval when you agree with something. Remember, what is important is not to be right but to improve your focus so you can achieve the result you desire; it is an inconvenience to tell other people they are wrong. Do not criticize, some other stubborn person will surely come and do it for you.

- When you give praises to someone, remember to point to the specific action for which you are doing it rather than to the person itself, otherwise your words may sound false.

- Do not complain. Most of the people do not care about

your troubles; they are so into themselves that they cannot hear you, while others may even be happy about your problems. It is more convenient to not complain about anything; besides, since energy is constantly retro-feeding itself, you may end up constantly filling yourself up with negativity.

- One of the keys to prosperity is to be grateful. Continually give thanks, both in public and in private, for any person who did something deserving of it. At the end of each day of your life and before going to sleep, it is appropriate to make sure your last thoughts are of giving thanks: go over the details of your day and you will find many reasons to be grateful, such as your life, the air you breathe, your family, your friends, your means of transportation, everything material, spiritual, and the blessings and lessons from the experiences you lived. A grateful heart will open the doors to unlimited prosperity.
- In your mind, get used to going over what your ideal day would look like; use your imagination to go over your day as you would have liked it to be, and not as it happened. With practice, and in some cases, your day will look more or less like what you imagine.
- When you go to an appointment or speak on the phone, say *hi* and begin by saying your name and then ask for the person you are looking for. This projects a proper sense of importance and self-esteem, so the person you speak to will understand he is talking to someone of importance.
- When you speak to another person, make sure that in your mind's eye you are both the same size If you are in front of someone who represents authority and prestige to you, elevate yourself mentally before opening your mouth; do it until you see yourself as big as the other person. If you are talking to someone you consider less important or of lesser means, use your mind to elevate that person and bring you both to the same level before you begin to speak to him. In the first case, the other person will perceive that you are

> confident and secure about yourself; this in turn will make you more credible. In the second case, the other person will feel respected and loved; you had the wisdom to see him as equal to you, as a result, this person will give his all to make things good for you.

– "Too much information." I said, and I was getting ready to elaborate on the idea but Mr. Deeb interrupted me.

– "Yes, and without having the opportunity to put it to the test it can give you a case of mental indigestion; like when you eat too much, it can do harm to your body. I suggest you look for someone you can teach what you have learned here to; teaching is one of the best ways to learn, because what we teach the best is what we need to learn the most about."

– "Even if all I can teach is theory, it does not matter?" I asked.

– "Yes," He said, "some people are at the level where theory alone will awake them. We will continue tomorrow."

I left the building in a hurry, looking for the person that would allow me to do my homework. I found a childhood friend with whom I found it easy to share all these theories because he barely paid attention to what I said. I was surprised to hear me speaking with such confidence about these subjects, and I thought to myself about all the people who spend their lives teaching about things they never put into practice; I noticed it all served a purpose, like a guinea pig that helped me to understand things better. I arrived very early to my next appointment with Mr. Deeb. This time no one waited for me; his assistant arrived about an hour later, and half an hour later my instruction resumed.

– "What happened with the whole thing about respecting other people's time?" That was the question I decided to begin with.

– "And what happened with being an active, receptive listener?" That was Mr. Deeb's answer. "You left in such a hurry, that we never got the chance to set up a time for our next appointment. You assume other people will tell themselves what you tell yourself. You left so wrapped up in your on world that you forgot we had not talked about a time. Now, let us take advantage of the time we have because every time we meet in the future we will have less time to share."

– "Oh! That sounds sad!" I reprimanded myself for the attitude I gave him at the beginning of our meeting, so I proceeded to take notes of his teachings.

– "Today, we will talk about two very important subjects in support of a proper attitude: self-esteem and self-image. I will give you some images to illustrate my point.

SELF-ESTEEM AND SELF-IMAGE

Humans, in their ignorance, tend to look at one another as it is reflected by those images: some are bigger and others are smaller; not in terms of height, but internally, in our inner dialogues.

Low self-esteem disguised as humbleness

The previous image shows the way you see yourself internally as being smaller than the other person. In general, this is due to low self-esteem and low self-image. In order for your word to be credible and respected, you need to equalize your self-image to that of the other person before your speak; a common mistake is to try and bring down the other person to the size of your own self-image, in which case the other person will feel disrespected.

When you become capable of equalizing your self-image to that of the person you speak with, you will convey confidence and security in the information you are sharing or in the relationship you are working on.

Low self-esteem disguised as arrogance

If the situation you are experiencing is the opposite from the previous one – as the image above shows – and your ego leads you to perceive yourself as bigger than the other person, unable to recognize that all human beings are equal by divine principle and created in the image of God, then the other person will feel humiliated and will not be able to fully express all of his potential.

In this case, you must mentally elevate the other person and bring him to your same level, this way he will feel loved and respected. Information will flow properly both ways and the dialogue or relationship will be easy. Never diminish your self-image in order to bring yourself to the level of the other person because a part of yours will feel disrespected and undervalued.

Proper self-esteem, proper humility

The proper way to communicate with others is just as it is represented in the previous figure; do not ever look at other people as being bigger or smaller than you. Always make sure you have either elevated yourself or elevate the other person before you talk to them. When you are able to elevate yourself and others, information flows more readily both ways, your self-esteem and self-image are just right, you are self-confident and live in an atmosphere of love and respect. Do this every time you relate to someone else; develop the ability to be at the same level as the other person no matter the circumstances and your relationships will be adequate and enjoyable; you will feel at ease and happy to share with people, while at the same time you will receive information from them that you may eventually need.

Pay attention to your thoughts every time you encounter someone, making sure you are having the right kind of thoughts about them; before talking to anybody, convince yourself this person in front of you is the most important person in the planet, because it really is so. Everybody likes to feel important and valued, and when you recognize you are being treated in such a way you immediately want the best for that person.

Self-esteem is directly related to worthiness, self-love, and is your way to establish what you deserve in the world; first, you improve your self-esteem and then your results will follow suit. Self-image, the twin sister of self-esteem, manifests how close you are to conquering your dreams. Self-esteem makes you feel like you deserve a certain car or house, or achieving your goals; self-image comes into action when you go to check out and test drive the car at the auto dealer, or when you go visit and take pictures of your dream house; when you can see, hear and feel yourself in possession of what you desire, as if it already is so, beyond temporary circumstances or limits of time or money. There are people with a high level of self-esteem but a very poor sense of self-image, as a result, they self-sabotage, which in turns prevents them from taking concrete actions both physically and mentally in order to achieve their dreams. Most of the people cannot fulfill their dreams because they feel incapable or unworthy, and they do not believe they deserve conquering their dreams or goals.

Self-esteem and self-image are very important in order to be successful because the way you feel about yourself is how others see and perceive you. The veracity of the information you provide depends highly on your level of self-esteem and self-image, and these depend on your level of self –confidence and how you see the person you are relating to. You have to be clear, you will never attract into your life any one thing above your levels of self-esteem and self-image; you need to continually work on improving these two qualities, and the way to do it is very simple: choose the information that makes you feel unique and special; read self-help books and listen to audio that helps you to believe in God, in yourself, in others and what you do.

The majority of people desire many things and even know how to properly formulate them; they could describe them to you with great detail - using their five senses - and tell you what they see, hear, smell and taste, and even the texture of what they desire; they would know how to tell you when, where and with who they want it; however, their days go by in despair because they cannot understand the reason their desires do not manifest quickly and easily. The reason being: many times and out of ignorance, we see other people as bigger or smaller than us, and we do the same thing with our dreams; we desire a car, a house or a farm, and even though we know exactly what we want, our internal dialogues perceive the dream as bigger than us. As a result, the only thing we get is that we unconsciously reject our desire and later cannot understand why we cannot satisfy our wishes.

The right step to take toward the materialization of our dreams is to observe our inner size when we think of obtaining such dreams, and then do the necessary adjustments in order to have the proper configuration or the right frame of mind that matches the size of our dream."

– "How could we achieve this?" I asked.

– "Let us assume you wish to have a car, latest model and the best brand; even though you know the color you like, the size and smell, when you want it, where and who you would like to share that dream with, your self-image is inferior to your desire and because of this every time you visualize yourself already having the car you see it as something far from your reach and unattainable. You need to adjust your self-image so that every time you see the car, it is the same size as yours; sometimes when you are dealing with physical dreams you tend to see the thing you desire, not as bigger or smaller than you, but as farther or closer to you. Usually, when your self-image is smaller than your dream, you tend to see the object of desire as distant, opaque and cold. A good strategy would be to bring it close to you; the inner distance at which you see the object is the same at which you usually have it once you own it, so give it enough light, the proper temperature and, in general, do anything that makes you feel like you already have it with a sense of happiness, with the certainty it is already coming into your life. It is important to change your mental programs and learn to feel worthy of everything you desire just as you are, without associating the conquest of your dream to the need to change something in you, or a certain area of your life.

Only you can choose how to think and feel in any given situation. Choose wisely in order for your internal dialogues to be right and to live in a permanent state of empowerment, consciously knowing that even though you may experience many things which may not be exactly to your liking, they are still important for your learning process and evolution; as such, putting them in their proper context helps in overcoming each experience more rapidly.

About empathy

There are nice or funny kinds of people, and they are called pleasant; others have the capacity to be obnoxious, inspire rejection, and are generally aggressive or live upset, and they are called unpleasant. A third group of people have the ability to see God in every person and relate to others as they relate to themselves, and these are called empathic.

The best way to define people who are capable of being empathic is like this: they are wise human beings with a proper sense of self-esteem and self-image, and they have the ability to be unnoticed. They feel and make others feel like equal human beings, striving to eliminate differences and taking pleasure in similarities. Remembering the words of a famous French designer: 'To be elegant is to be unnoticed, but when noticed it is unforgettable.' The effort to be pleasant is interpreted by the subconscious as a person whose message cannot be trusted; as a result, it turns into an unpleasant person."

– "How can one generate empathy?" I inquired.

– "The ability to generate empathy is of utmost importance in order to achieve proper communication. Empathy can be generated by means of verbal (words), and non-verbal communication (gestures). Most of the times you do not need to do anything, for it just happens naturally and spontaneously. When it happens, you need to establish a proper communication link; it is important to be able to generate an environment of empathy, and this can be instituted by agreeing with the other person on a subject, having something in common or by a combination of verbal and non-verbal elements of communication and experience. The following are some verbal and nonverbal signs to give to the unconscious:

- To speak in the same channel or sensory sequence as your interlocutor; what this means is that if the person is using visual (I see, brilliant, dark, colorful, landscape), auditory (I hear, rhythm, repeat, listen to me, echo, silence, whisper) or kinetic words (rough, sweet, hard, soft, I feel, reject), you use that same channel of communication.
- Make the tone and volume of your voice equal or as close to that of your interlocutor; if the person speaks fast, you do the same; is they speak loud, so do you and vice versa. Keep in mind the following: if the person feels imitated you will get the opposite effect, meaning you will be rejected. As a result, you must be careful and learn to control well this technique.
- Every so often, use the same filler words the other person is using. It is very common for people to use a certain filler word or slang depending on where they live; these words are very common for some people but not for others. For example: cool, buddy, mate, bro, among many others.
- Adjust the position of your body so it imitates or resembles your interlocutor's; a body posture that looks similar to that of the other person you are speaking with generates a sense of trust.
- Use gestures equal or similar to those of your interlocutor's. The same goes for your facial expressions.

On the other hand, other times you will need to be antipathetic in order to avoid creating empathy with things or experiences you do not wish to have. If you do not wish to celebrate a certain situation that makes all the other people laugh, it might be appropriate and important for you to show a serious expression. If on some special occasion – or due to some job related or charitable activities – you wind up going to a prison or jail, you will need to generate some antipathy towards the fact you are entering such a place. One way to do it is by being in that world but not being of it, focusing on the service you give to others and the solutions you offer to their problems, rejecting the way people live in that world.

Become an observer of what you are attracting into your life; in order to achieve this, the question you must ask yourself is the following: To who or what am I becoming attractive? Then, generate a state of empathy with what you like, and a state of antipathy with all you desire to eliminate from your existence.

When you observe what you are bringing into your life with the keen eye of a detective, you can become responsible for it.

There are two types of person in life: those who live in the world feeling they are victims of destiny — which can in fact be called an illusion — and those who recognize they are the creators of their circumstances and face them head on in order to change their results. The first ones believe in luck, and this is no more than the crossing point between opportunity and preparation; when they ignore this fact, their lives lack will power. Imagine wanting to change a movie by attempting to manipulate the screen on which it is being projected... it would be absurd. Changes do not happen at the screen; if you desire to change the movie of your life, change the recordings that are creating your present arguments. The second kind of people recognize themselves as the absolute creators of their results, knowing the universe supports them unconditionally in the pursuit of what they wish to believe in and create. They are not brought down by circumstances; when they do not like a result, they take them apart in order to go in and recreate a new argument, manifesting the reality of their world through mental images, visualization of the successful result and through the use of their word, becoming conscious of every decree they make. They know their results are the product of what they have and have not done in their lives.

The best way to discover what you are consciously and unconsciously creating is by examining what you are attracting into your life. Nothing happens by chance; everything obeys the laws of cause and effect, so everything happens by causality. Observe, without making judgments, what you constantly attract into your life: some people attract people who humiliate them and others who praise them; some attract health and others sickness and accidents; some attract richness and others poverty and debt; other people attract love, realization and happiness, while others attract loneliness, sadness and rejection. Regardless of what you attract, as soon as you realize it, observe whether you like or not what is coming into your life. If you do not like it, it is important to reprogram yourself in order to attract new results."

– "And the way to do it is just as with the road of success?" I asked Mr. Deeb, knowing my question would make me detour from the most important subject I have ever studied in my life; lessons so simple yet so powerful, that to put them into practice would become an urgent and important matter to accomplish in my life.

– "Exactly the same;" he said, "if you desire to change what you attract into your life, you need to change your internal dialogues. In order to do that you need to change your beliefs, which in turn are changed by feeding yourself new information, and you achieve this by controlling what you get in through your five senses."

– "It sounds very easy. Who would have though the information we receive can have such an impact in our lives." I said.

– "This is the time for humanity to become conscious of their mental programs, and of the huge impact the things they receive through their five senses have in their lives." Said Mr. Deeb.

– "I have heard the first law of the spirit is acceptance, so when I generate antipathy, am I not violating that principle?"

– "No." He replied. "The concepts of reprogramming yourself and acceptance are very different from one another: to accept that the circumstances you attract into your life where created by you and to recognize you need to change many of the things you did in order to obtain those results, otherwise you will continue to live the same things over and over. Be antipathetic toward the things you do not wish to continue creating or attracting into your reality; the right way to do it is by creating new thoughts that focus your attention on the life style you wish to live, avoiding to fall prey to the old ways of thinking and the temptation to abandon what you really desire. If for some reason that causes you grief you wish to put distance between you and a certain person, give up any kind of information that connects you to such person; instead of concentrating on not thinking about the person, you must think about other people who bring happiness into your life."

– "How amazing to think about the power attitudes can have over our lives!" I said to Mr. Deeb. "It seems that by working on them we end up giving up the need to be right. Sometimes I get the feeling this whole thing about working consciously on our attitudes in order to direct our results sounds a bit forced, as if we have to pretend to be something that we are not, why is that? In some cases I would even feel like I am being dishonest, like smiling without an apparent reason. I think that to change the context of our experiences simply leads to undervaluing what we really feel."

– "I have repeatedly said the same to you over the course of our interviews, that our mission is to learn, grow and change. One of the greatest dilemmas a person experiences when wishing to enter the road to excellence is that constant need to be right versus the desire to obtain the results they want; sooner or later, you will realize the only valid option is to choose the results and leave behind the need to be right. What a difference it would make if people chose to take into consideration the experiences of all the great men to have ever walked on this planet, such as Buddha, Confucius, Plato, Jesus Christ, Muhammad, Shakespeare, Gandhi, Mother Theresa of Calcutta, Pope John Paul II and many more! They all left us with great teachings, among them not to take things too seriously, giving in to small things; they all knew their time here was counted and now they are gone from this planet, just as it will happen to you and me. Always make sure small things do not get in the way of the conquest, the mandates, and the true desires of your heart.

One way to show how much you value your existence is by consciously choosing how to feel with any given experience that you live; what this means is, once you realize that life is short, you will focus on enjoying your circumstances while recognizing everything that happens to you is for your own learning process. No matter how much you work on improving your attitudes, it will never be enough; the more you work on them, the more dominion over yourself you will have. You are embarking upon the greatest conquest of them all, the only one that matters, and that is the conquest of your own self.

About behavior

Now, let us analyze behaviors, which are a direct result of our attitudes."

– "Behavior," I thought out loud, as if the concept did not need much explanation, however, I connected with a question that would allow me to learn something new about it. "What is behavior?" I asked, but then I was left thinking to myself maybe this question will not necessarily lead to an empowering answer.

– "It is the way you act under all circumstances." Responded Mr. Deeb.

– "What is the difference between attitude, inner dialogues and behavior?"

– "Behavior is the conclusion or the result of the other two. Proper inner dialogues generate a great attitude, and these two together invite you to behave the right way. When your inner dialogues govern the way to feel or behave in a certain situation, you own your destiny and consciously choose your behavior. This is typical behavior of those who possess character and truly own themselves; their focus is oriented toward getting the results they want. On the other hand, when the external situation has dominion over your internal dialogues, hence determining the way you feel, you become a victim of circumstances, like a puppet whose strings are pulled by the external. Most of the people opt for the second choice, usually those wishing to be right."

– "Could you please illustrate this idea with an example?" I requested Mr. Deeb.

– "Let us assume you are going to exercise and the morning is a bit rainy and cold; you have two options: in the first one, your internal dialogue tells you to go immediately and do your exercises for which your body goes along with your decision, so you are living from the inside out, doing your own will. In the second option, you observe the circumstances of the day and choose not to fulfill your inner wish; instead, you decide to occupy yourself on something else with the excuse that the circumstances of the day do not support what you desire.

The key is to win in your fantasies; every human creation process starts with a fantasy, something we judge as unreal, untrue, an illusion. You win in your fantasies when you consciously choose what is possible or not for you to accomplish beyond external appearances. Although it may sound illogical, most people give up their dreams because in their fantasies they are losers; before they begin the project or before taking action, they tell themselves they will lose and because of that they become a failure. Given the option to believe or not to believe, to feel you can win or lose, to know you can or cannot perform, you have the power to choose to win or lose in your fantasies; neither option is real, however, choosing to win puts you in a better position, filled with energy, enthusiasm and optimism. To think it is impossible to fail is to win in your fantasies, is like going to the future in order to create the present moment with the certainty of success.

A lot of people work very hard and never know why they cannot get the results they desire: if they were to carefully analyze their situation, they would realize the problem is with their behavior that unconsciously repels what they so eagerly desire."

– "How could we improve on our behavior?"

– "The key word is enthusiasm: it comes from *entheus* or to live in God, and this is the energy that propels people to follow you, but it is also a synonym for good news. Every enthusiastic person is a happy person, committed, determined, and is perceived by others as someone who knows where he is going. People like to be in the presence of an enthusiastic person."

– 'What techniques are there to help increase one's levels of enthusiasm?" I asked.

– "Many," he said, "and among the most effective ones there is the ability to dream big, to know exactly what you desire in life; to accept what happens knowing you can change the future by means of what you do here and now. Begin to practice the following simple, yet effective technique: in a notebook, write down your dreams and all positive situations you experience, like a diary of good news; with as many details as possible, narrate every aspect of the dream or situation that brings about the feeling of good news, and then re-read it when you need some self-motivation or in order to improve your enthusiasm; just as ignorance reduces our enthusiasm, to remember and know produces enthusiasm. If you wish to become enthusiastic about visiting another country, find out as much information about it and in short time you will be enthusiastic about the country. Lack of knowledge about a certain kind of business makes it uninteresting to you, but to acquire knowledge about it fills you with enthusiasm for it. It is almost as if information brings things into life, while the lack of it just kills them inside of us because we ignore t heir existence. The same thing happens with a person: if you desire to become enthusiastic about a person, get to know him as best you can; and if your aim is a certain subject, get as much information as possible about it.

The more information, the more enthusiasm; the less information, the less interest; you choose the behavior you display at any given moment of your life. In order to achieve the behavior you desire you need to work in your Being, and that will lead you mainly to react unconsciously in the most effective way, besides giving you the opportunity to discover yourself as an unlimited being limited only by yourself, by your beliefs, your information, and by the knowledge that enters your Being through your five senses.

I will tell you a story. Once upon a time, a disciple went and visited his master teacher, the great wise man of the town, with the intention of discovering the key to prosperity. For this, he asked the man to provide him with all the information he had on the subject of prosperity and abundance. Without thinking twice about it, the master teacher proceeded immediately to give him books, not necessarily about the subject he requested, but on the subject of wisdom. He invited the disciple to read the books and come back the next year. On the next year, the disciple came back very proud of himself and told him he had read every single book and that if he, the master teacher, could now provide him with the books on the subject of prosperity; next thing you know, the master teacher gave him more books on wisdom and recommended that he read them and come back the next year. This went one for several years, until one day the disciple became so interested in wisdom that by the time he came back to see the teacher he asked if he could give him more books on wisdom; once the master teacher saw this, he proceeded to give him all the books he possessed on the sacred keys to prosperity."

– "What a beautiful story!" I exclaimed. "What I understand is that true prosperity comes as a result of working in our Being, in knowing how to Be."

– "Yes," Said Mr. Deeb "the road to prosperity and the conquest of our dreams or goals, however you wish to call them, happens by means of working on our Being; more important than achieving an objective, is the kind of person we turn into as a result of the conquest of that dream. A very effective way to work on our Being is by asking God to illuminate you and turn you into a secure, loving, creative, humble, wise, happy, giving, perseverant, constant, determined, honest, disciplined, patient, charitable, enthusiastic, and optimistic - and all the other qualities of the Being - kind of person. This means, to search for the kingdom of God and all the other things will be added unto you. Remember the phrase: 'Ask and it shall be given.' The shortest road between where you stand now and the realization of your deepest desires is to work on developing all these qualities, and you already know that in order to achieve it you must fill yourself with all the information you can get regarding each one of them. When you focus on each one of these qualities, you will begin to be impregnated by the same kind of information and energy until the day you realize they have become an intrinsic part of your being.

From another stand point, it would seem as if the reason you come to this planet is so you can transform yourself, to overcome your current state of enslavement, or how conditioned by the seven deadly sins you live; your task is to turn each one of them into a quality or cardinal virtue.

Seven Deadly Sins	Seven Cardinal Virtues
Pride	Humility
Greed	Charity
Lust	Chastity
Anger	Patience
Sloth	Diligence
Envy	Kindness
Gluttony	Temperance

To go from walking the path of the deadly sins to the path of the cardinal virtues is a true life's purpose, one that fills you with a sense of inner conquest and authentic realization; it is a life of permanent and fulfilling success in which you are ready to achieve anything you want. The wisdom of life invites you to know how *to be* in order to know how *to do*, to know what it is *to have*. When you constantly work in the Being you become coherent an efficient at doing things, and with that, you get what you want without limits; all your dreams come true when you live working in the Being. The problem is that the majority of people apply this route backwards: first, they desire to have things, ignoring they will not take any of it when they leave this plane; then, they do desire to do things in order to be. It is a big mistake to desire to have cars and luxurious houses in order to do as you please without regard and be Mr. or Mrs. So and So."

– "That is what most of humanity do." I said.

– "Yes, and they usually live as they can afford rather than as they would like to; their dreams become unattainable fantasies because they take the wrong road. If you are in Central America and you go to the South, you will reach Argentina; if you go to the North you end up in Canada; the right road leads you to the desire objective. You already know the key lies in following the road of success, step by step, knowing exactly what you want and controlling the information you receive, and all that will undoubtedly lead you to display the proper behavior. You can learn as much from your own experiences as from other people's; that in turn speeds up your learning process, and it is the reason why modeling or imitating other people is so in vogue. First, you determine exactly what you want. Then, you check and see who has already achieved that result; and lastly, you begin to model that person's strategy. Now, if what you want is to go pass the surface and into the heart of things, you could ask the person you selected to model what kind of information he uses to feed his mind; the more you feed yourself the same kind of information, the faster you will get the results you desire."

– "Are you trying to say that more than just modeling the other person's beliefs and attitudes, it is more convenient to know the kind of information he feeds his mind and begin to feed the same to mine? And if I do that, my beliefs and attitudes will sooner or later be the same as those of the person I am modeling?" I asked Mr. Deeb.

– "Exactly." Replied Mr. Deeb. "People wish to learn how to obtain other people's results, but they fail to accomplish it because they focus on modeling the consequence instead of the cause. I know it is very clear to you by now that the raw material from which we build our dreams lies in the information we receive through our five senses."

– "Is there some kind of information that is more powerful than other?" I wondered out loud.

– "Yes. There is a kind of information which creates what is known as *regent thoughts*, and I talked to you about them on a previous interview. These thoughts or beliefs have a greater impact on your results, and all the other thoughts are subordinated to them. The moment you try to do something contrary to what your regent thoughts say is when you fall into self-sabotage. Let me say it more clearly: if, on the one hand, you desire to start a company that will create products which will be harmful to the environment and, on the other hand, you have a regent thought demanding that you take care of nature, even if the company is a complete success you will find an unconscious way to bring it down. If your regent thought is trying to get you to earn your way to heaven, and in order to do that you need to be poor, the moment prosperity comes into your life you will push it away.

There are three types of regent thoughts:

1. Personal Lie, created at conception and during gestation.

2. Beliefs about God or your religious education.

3. Generalized belief about what is true and what is not; these are stipulated by people who represent a figure of power, authority or wisdom for each specific person.

Every time you do something contrary to one of your regent thoughts, you self-sabotage and self-punish. The regent thought brings all the other thoughts under its ruling thumb. The majority of people do not even know what their regent thoughts are, and this is what gets in their way on a day to day basis; if there is something they are trying to do which contravenes one of their regent thoughts, they will never achieve their objectives; something will happen just in time to deviate them from the conquest of their dream. If you wish to conquer your dreams, and your did what was necessary but you did not achieve it, you need to evaluate yourself and find out whether you need to change a regent thought that is getting in the way of what you desire. Not all regent thoughts are negative. On the contrary, they are in charge of keeping you alive, living a fulfilling and happy life at all levels: spiritual, mental and material. It just so happens that sometimes we have chosen a virus to be one of our regent thoughts. Some of the viruses that pose as a regent thoughts are the following: 'I am worthless, I am no good, I am not desired, I am rejected, I cannot do it, I am incapable, I am a fraud, I am bad.' To have any or many of these beliefs as a regent thought is a serious problem, as they block your ability to easily conquer your dreams."

— "At what moment do we receive such negative information? Moreover, why does it have such impact in our lives?"

— "Regent thoughts known as *the personal lie* or *greater limitation* are the result of the unconscious conclusion that we reach after the experiences we lived when we were conceived, while we were in our mother's womb and at the moment of birth. What our parents thought or felt was recorded in our cells, it is what is called cellular memory; we accept all of those premises as being true, only because at that time we were unable to discern."

— "How can these regent thoughts turn out to be so different from one person to another?" I asked.

— "Let us assume your parents did not want to have children, and then you were conceived as an accident; the negative regent thought is one of 'I am not desired,' and as a result you will live many experiences of rejection, or you may conclude that you are not loved or that you are not worthy. If you desired to have a boy and instead you had a girl, the girl may conclude she is a fraud or that she does not deserve the good things in life, or she may simply believe that she is a letdown. These are just some examples and it does not mean they are exactly like that, what is important is to find the virus conditioning your current results. A positive regent thought is to think God is in charge of everything, and everything happens for our own good because we deserve the best.

If you think in terms of what is valuable to a person, whatever holds the most value in their scale turns into a regent thought, and all other thoughts become subject to it. The good news is you have the power to choose and change your regent thoughts as you see fit; you just need to identify them and verify whether they work for you or not, and if the answer is no, then change them. To be observant will help you identify them; be always vigilant about the things you attract into your life, therein lies the key to change your results. Sometimes, you will need to focus on finding and transforming your regent thoughts, in other words, your paradigms. People who create their prosperity at the expense of harming others, and quickly turn to spend it or throw it away, unknowingly make use of a positive regent thought that says *money must be earned right.*"

— "Is there such thing as a value scale that would allow me to verify which thought is subject to others?"

– "The scale to determine the value of information is this: information that nurtures you spiritually conditions the information that nurtures mind; information that nurtures your mind conditions your physicality; all of these condition your relationships, your work, financial status, physical body, spiritual relationship, your lessons and the way you choose to entertain yourself."

– "In other words, spiritual information is the most important one, is that right?"

– "It may be even more powerful than you are capable of understanding right this moment. If people were conscious of how delicate the spiritual information they receive is, and of the impact it has in their lives, they would be more inclined to choose more wisely what and who they read or listen to. Most spiritual leaders educate their followers through fear, the idea of the punishing God and manipulation, interpreting the sacred texts they work with in whichever manner suits them most; they use the individual and collective ignorance as a tool to make them feel guilty and unworthy of enjoying the life they deserve by the mere fact of being alive, and by forgetting to mention this one basic premise: we are all made in God's image. A true spiritual guide's purpose is to make his followers understand it is impossible to be separate from God and that He, in His infinite wisdom, created the universe and a set of perfect, unmovable laws so that everything happens in perfect order; laws that will take us by the hand in order to lead us from our ignorance toward wisdom, from darkness to light, and then everything that is not love needs to be brought out in order to be healed. Whenever you receive spiritual information, you need to turn on your antivirus and check that it is being taught through love, acceptance and forgiveness. Once you are done receiving such information, make sure that you feel empowered, filled with the desire to live, to do well, and that your are filled with the spirit of God."

– "How do I know I am filled with the spirit of God?" I asked.

– "Even though is difficult to explain the experience, there are some signs which allow us to know that indeed we are filled with the spirit of God. More than just happiness, you feel a great sense of joy and peace; a desire to be a better person, to help improve our environment and our relations; a great love fills your heart, as well as a profound feeling that nothing is impossible. The most important thing is to feel, with all certainty, that the person serving as your spiritual guide is not the one talking, but that he is only being used by Spirit; and without knowing how to explain it, you recognize the special message from God being delivered to you through this person and the information you are receiving."

– "You are right." I said. "I never thought spiritual information could have such power to condition us."

– "It is not spiritual information that conditions us, but rather the pseudo-spiritual communicator who does."

– "I do not understand."

– "A person may believe that he is serving as a channel for spirit to bring information to humans, but what he does is he perpetuates himself, his fears or paradigms."

– "How do I know I have the right kind of guide?"

– "You may identify him by the results you obtain; remember to always keep in mind that the task of being a messenger of spiritual information is a privilege which must be earned day by day. Spirit may choose to use a certain person today but not tomorrow, simply because the person may no longer be living in a rightful way. Many times, personality gets in the way and those who think themselves the messengers of spirit end up preaching through their ego or pride. True spiritual guides are very clear about this, so they work ardently through meditation, prayer, contemplation and many other spiritual practices, in order to keep themselves in check and prevent their personalities from getting in the way of delivering a clear message. In order for the right information to come to you at the right moment, and in order for you to have an attitude of understanding and comprehension, you may want to put yourself in the light and put the person who will be delivering spirit's message in the light as well."

– "Which religion is the right one, the one that holds the truth and that is the most convenient for me?"

– "All and none," He replied. "The same religion that helps one person to evolve spiritually, may do nothing for someone else; another person may feel it does nothing for their personal growth and that it is not their path; once you choose a certain one to be your own spiritual path you must follow it to the letter, otherwise you will self-sabotage continually or even come up with different ways to punish yourself. You should not worry about this, once you find the right religion for you, the one to be your spiritual path, you will know it within yourself."

– "What if the person does not belong to a particular religion? What creates the regent thoughts then?"

– "First and foremost, through the genetic information we receive from our parents with regards to that subject, and then when we reach the age at which our discernment becomes null and everything we hear becomes the word of God." Said Mr. Deeb.

– "What age is that?"

– "From the time you are in your mother's womb until you reach seven years of age. Throughout life, we receive religious information from different sources; afterwards, when we are able to discern and as we choose not to follow a specific religion and begin to understand more about the spiritual laws, these become our regent thoughts; they are thirty three immutable laws that cannot be changed. Then you come to understand that your body is the temple and the light is inside our heart."

– "I feel you are not answering my question." I said.

– "You are internally drawn to follow the pre-established laws of the universe. These are the true regent thoughts; everything else is just a temporary belief in the search for the eternal. A good use of time would be for you to do a complete analysis of your regent thoughts and determine which ones are limiting and which ones empower you. Furthermore, one day you will be able to go beyond those laws just because of your complete knowledge of and willingness to follow and obey them, and you will live in that state of grace in which everyone desires to live. When you live in grace you come from a state of joy; miracles happen right and left; nobody is judged, you simply observe everything and everyone with a sense of acceptance; and you live from the inside out, creating exactly what you want in your environment.

Later on, after you come to understand the workings of the regent thoughts, you will need to learn about a second category of thoughts you also have: *conditioning thoughts*. Conditioning thoughts set limits between what can and cannot be, what you can and cannot learn, what you can or cannot have and what you can or cannot mentally or physically do. It is important to recognize you chose to have these limiting thoughts, and if you want you, you can also change them because they keep you tied to your current results. When your physical body does not support you, or the material results that you are getting are not the ones you desire, you need to double check on your thoughts; make whatever changes are necessary because they are the ones that create and subordinate everything material. Your mind changes your physical reality, and if your mind loses control over your physicality or your physical desires rule your life, go to your spirit, for it is there where you will find the power to change and direct your thoughts.

Up until now, the road to success shows us the importance of establishing clear objectives and controlling the information we receive: the next lesson has to do with mastery. Study and go over your notes; apply them so you can put them to the test and verify, through experience, whether they work or not. I will see you next week."

– "Thank you very much, I have learned so many things and I feel so happy that I wish our meetings would never end, but I understand everything has its time, so I will be happily looking forward to our next appointment. Until then, Mr. Deeb." I finally said.

– "Go with God, may He bless you. Remember, do not allow your past experiences to condition your current attitudes and the way you conduct yourself."

I left the place, but first I made sure the next appointment's time and date were clearly established; I knew without a shadow of a doubt I was receiving key information, one that would help me for the rest of my life. It was so much information that I felt confused by the fact I was not putting it into practice right away; the sensation resembled indigestion, except this time it was mental indigestion.

During that time, I wondered what it would be like if we were taught the principles of success from an early age, what the planet would be like if we were taught such basic and obvious things that I find it hard to understand the reason we do not do it. I wanted to change my results immediately, all at once; why wait? This formula would allow me to become an example of life to many people who, out of their own ignorance, fail to obtain what they desire and almost always blame it on divine will, as if God were some kind of dictator of the universe lacking in equality and enjoying punishing some and rewarding others without rhyme or reason.

What a mistake; God created us all in his image, of equal essence from birth and with the right to be unequal; common people obtaining common results and common people obtaining extraordinary results. The only difference residing in our decision to go the extra mile, and I would also add this, that you go the extra mile the right way, or better, the wise and right way, doing more of what actually works."

"We are what we do on a daily basis.

PART FIVE

Given this, excellence is not an act but a habit."
Aristotle

THE POWER OF CONTINUOUS AND PERSEVERING ACTION

I spent the whole week in introspection, having major realizations and experiencing a great desire to be grateful and committed. Without knowing why, I was finding it hard to sleep on the eve of my next meeting with Mr. Deeb; I felt a sense of peace come over me when I noticed the first rays of the sun appearing in the sky, and I rushed to get ready for what I considered would be a very special day. I arrived thirty minutes in advance to our meeting, hoping I would be able to spend more time with Him, but he was engaged with other people and we ended up meeting at the exact time we had agreed.

– "Good morning, Mr. Deeb!" I said, greeting him with a profound sense of love and happiness that seemed to come from the very bottom of my soul; without having to speak a word, I sensed he was in somewhat of a hurry, like wishing to make the most of every minute of our time.

– "Good morning, son! How was your week?" He asked.

– "Excellent, I was very happy and I pondered a lot. I am beginning to understand that in order to put all of these information into practice requires great responsibility, and that might be the way I will contribute to better the world, through my example."

– "You have said it yourself." Said Mr. Deeb. "The most important thing is to set the example; 'Only knowledge that is applied persists in the spirit;' I read that phrase a long time ago in a self-help book, and every time I find it to be more and more valid. These last few days I thought about our last conversation, and I realized that in our last session I forgot to talk to you about the invisible guides. The knowledge of all times is always available to anyone who wants to use it. From the highest forms of thought to the lowest ones, the route followed by both the greatest of scholars and wise men, as well as the most perverse and horrible people in this world in order to achieve their results...all of that knowledge is available to everyone. If you learn to connect with the memory of the days, you will surely realize that in the end you really are a connector. According to your level of vibration, you consciously connect with invisible worlds from where you get information, to the point sometimes you do not even know whether you are thinking or some other entity is thinking of you."

– "Everything impacts our lives." I thought to myself, trapped in my own inner dialogues.

– "Yes," Said Mr. Deeb, even though I never even opened my mouth. "Right this moment you and I are able to connect at the same frequency, and if we wish to, we can also do it telepathically, meaning, you can hear my thoughts and I can hear yours. This happens very often, although we are not always conscious of it; a very simple example would be when you think about someone and then the person calls you, or you call someone that has just been thinking about you; it would appear as if you had the intention to call when in reality you were answering to a thought sent by the other person. Most people are not aware of this, so they think it is just a coincidence, or that it is in their minds - whether it is for doing good or evil - not knowing that in reality they are being influenced by external energies that invite them to act in one way or another. Now that you are beginning to work with this knowledge, you may start to consciously choose who to connect with and select your invisible guides. Some of them taught you as a baby, while you were in your crib and your parents invoked the angels to protect or illuminate you; they stopped doing it later on in your life."

– "And why was that?" I asked.

– "Because your parents are being guided to call those guides to you during that first stage of your life, unbeknownst to them. The important thing is that, from today on, you will be able to choose consciously your own guides. It is very easy to work with them; you only need to manifest your intention to do it. Just out of curiosity, before you go to bed or first thing when you get up in the morning, invoke the guidance of a guardian angel, tell him: 'for the greater good and the highest of ends, I invoke the angel of prosperity,' or the angel of love, health or wisdom, and you only just need to be open and receptive, without forcing anything to happen, and you will see what a difference it will make in your life."

– "Are these invisible guides the same as the angels?"

– "Not just them. You can connect with many other beings. Sometime ago in Santiago de Chile, father Alberto Hurtado had achieved his canonization by selecting Jesus Christ as his invisible guide; the way he connected with Christ's consciousness was through prayer, and every time he faced a dilemma his question was: 'What would Christ do in my place?' The right answer always came to him from within, and he put it into practice achieving the greatest level of transcendence in his life."

– "What is the procedure to access all of that information?" I wondered.

– "The scholars have called it cosmic memory, universal mind, collective unconscious; beyond names and labels, it keeps a record of every experience and knowledge acquired by every person who has ever existed. So, all your knowledge and abilities will also become part of the common pool of knowledge of life. At any given moment, during the whole of eternity, if a person desires to know what it would be like to have a certain experience all they need to do is connect with the collective unconscious and ask how would such a person react to that specific thing. This allows them to connect beyond limits of time and space and download the information. You may choose a person to be your guide, regardless of whether this person is still alive or not. In reality, it is your unconscious communicating with the collective unconscious and you perceive the information through your own thoughts."

— "Are you saying we can choose people that are no longer alive to be our role models of excellence? And that when we can ask questions and receive the answers through our own thoughts?"

— "I will explain it to you with an example: let us suppose you like to practice martial arts and you choose Bruce Lee to be your role model of excellence. You will realize that your current physical shape presents a bit of a limitation; overweight, elasticity or potency. You sit down and adopt a comfortable position, of preference with your eyes closed; you say a prayer in order to put yourself in the light and asking that all your experience happens for the greater good and the highest of ends. Then, you invoke the presence of Mr. Bruce Lee and imagine he is right in front of you, and so you ask him the questions you want. What will happen next is that the answer to your problem will arise from within you; you may believe that it is you who is coming up with it, however, the wisdom in the answers will attest to the fact you are being assisted by the entity you invoked."

— "I still don't understand how I could possibly connect with people that are still alive, and even less how it is that I can communicate with people who already died." I replied in confusion.

— "Your unconscious mind is permanently connected with the mind of every human being, meaning, the unconscious mind is one and all thoughts and experiences related to how every single person that exists and has ever existed has obtained their results are recorded in it. What you are learning now is how to communicate with the unconscious mind and to choose the specific kind of information that you need. The unconscious mind is like a database where you can find all the answers that you are looking for. However, our ignorance of its existence prevents us from utilizing all of that information."

— "Is this the reason some people swear they have seen or spoken to an angel, a saint or some person from the past?"

— "Yes," Said Mr. Deeb. "It is highly probable that the more we invoke a certain entity, the more likely it is that we will be able to get in contact with the image the entity had in life. Some people become fanatics or followers of certain people who have already passed; such is the case of Jose Gregorio Hernández, a great doctor invoked by many to ask for his assistance. The problem is when people become dependent on these entities, whether they are still alive or dead. What I want you to learn has nothing to do with these kinds of situations; the idea is not to become dependent on anything or anyone. Although you are invoking your invisible guide, what you are really doing is connecting to a specific file in the archives of the unconscious, and that file contains a record of the information you require. In other words, you do not want to communicate with that specific person, you are only using the entity's name as a key to access the specific file in the collective unconscious that contains the information that you are looking for.

All thoughts that have ever been created throughout eternity, by every single person to have ever existed throughout time, along with all the experiences they lived in order to solve every single problem or issue they had throughout their lives, they have all been recorded in the Akashic records or the collective unconscious. We can all access this information bank by using a key or code which consists of invoking the presence or name of the person we have chosen as our role model or invisible guide. More than just pretending to communicate with this entity, what we really do is we use the information, experience and wisdom they left recorded in the archive."

– "Are you saying that with each experience I live as I solve my own problems, I am creating my own file?"

– "Exactly. If you take a moment to analyze it, you will notice that at birth, neither you nor anybody else starts from zero; we use the wisdom of our ancestors and then we contribute the wisdom obtained from our experiences to the collective unconscious. The question we could ask ourselves is this: Do we represent a model that someone might want to imitate? If the answer is no, then we should make an effort to improve ourselves, so we can make a significant contribution to this world."

– "Forgive me for repeating myself, but I would like to understand this: If I desire to learn music or play the piano, I could invoke Beethoven; or if I wish to learn physics I could invoke Einstein; or if I desire to learn about love I can invoke Mother Theresa or Jesus Christ; and by invoking any of them, is not that they appear to me but that I bring myself to the timeless, space-less place in eternity where they existed, and once there I can access the information contained in that place. This will allow me to think like they would think and act like they would act under the circumstances I may be right at that moment?"

– "Yes, all of that is true. The majority of people go through life without using, not only their full potential, but all the potential of the experiences accumulated throughout eternity and that are contained in the collective unconscious. You also need to learn that human beings are in a continuous process of growth and evolution, and only when we are ready we can connect with new information. Evidently, when we discover it, we get the feeling that we have wasted a lot of time. The important thing is to realize that thanks to each previous lesson we are now ready to learn new ones. Remember how things were back in school? First, they taught you the letters, then words and sentences, and as time went by you learned to read.

Each step you take in life brings you to a new and greater level of understanding, and absolutely every experience is just as important whether we consider it to be right or wrong, because they will be the point of reference that will allow other humans to advance even faster. We are witnesses to the fact that with each passing day the world moves forward and evolves at a faster pace, and it is all as a result of having more access to the information and experiences left by others. When you advance the cosmos advances, and if you become stagnant you are robbing humanity of the right to be enriched by your experiences."

– "How can I make use of the Akashic record and connect with people that are still alive?"

– "You do it the same way. The collective unconscious is always recording and lives in the eternal present moment, so it matters not at what moment of eternity the person you desire to connect with lives or not. Invoke the person's name, feel his presence and ask your questions as if you were in front of each other; observe the answers that come to you without questioning them. For now just do it because therein lies the key. When you try to intellectualize the information, your mind goes into what is known as paralysis by analysis; a lot of people spend much time analyzing everything, and because of this they never take action, ignoring that information without action only works to inflate the ego. What is really important is to put the theory into action, and that is where the mastery resides.

Your behavior is conditioned by so many things! It is very important for you to know that what you think, say, feel, do and the way you nourish your spirit, mind and body, it is all reflected in your body. Your body gives you away; wherever you go you carry the memory of your life and this is the reason someone could conclude a lot of things about you upon first meeting."

– "But they can be wrong..." I argued.

– "That is true. However, in the majority of the cases their appreciations are correct. A question that will help you discern by yourself is this one: *How am I perceived by others?* You know, what you think you project through your physical image is very different from what people actually perceive from you. Listen carefully to what they say about you; a lot of it is mere projections from the person that is talking to you; when more than one person says the same about you, then and only then can you realize how other people perceive you, and that is a great piece of information that forces you to change your physical posture, and with that you will be able to change the way you feel and how you are perceived by others. It is a very different thing to look at a person whose back is straight, walks with resolve and talks fast and dynamic, from someone whose back is all bent, walks slowly and speaks slow and weak. Try it! Keep in mind how others perceive you so you can see how your body gives you away; ask yourself what you are identifying with. If you identify yourself with your children, your life will become senseless the moment they leave to go do their thing in this world; if it is your job that you identify with, you will be left hanging when do not have it anymore; if you identify with your body, you will be in trouble when you grow old."

— "Then, what should I identify myself with?" I asked puzzled.

— "Before even identifying yourself with something, it is more important to be clear about a couple of certain things. First, everything is temporary, everything changes, and nothing is permanent. Months ago these meetings did not exist in your life, now you have become attached to them, but at some point they will end. Everything is borrowed; you are the main character in the movie of your life, but that is all it is, a part in a movie. Second, what you really are is light, an infinite being, unlimited, immortal, omnisapient, omnipotent and omnipresent. Identify yourself with those qualities and you will stop suffering; life will stop happening to you and you will begin to enjoy it.

I told you how our physical bodies give us away, and just by taking one look at someone you can easily tell many things about their personal history, whether they are happy or not, whether they are successful or not, if they have a good sense of self-image and whether they are happy with themselves. You must know that even though we are the makers of our own destiny, builders of our future, the environment in which we live can have a major influence on us. I spoke to you about all the humans that live asleep, who allow everything external to have dominion over their destiny, and I also told you about those who are awake and they influence their environment, making things happen. Today I must clarify something: there are recordings that have the power to influence you greatly with all kinds of feelings, such as sadness, depression, hopelessness, or it can go the other way to happiness and optimism. These are known as ectoplasm. Ectoplasm is a kind of energy that surrounds all bodies and it is called by different names: sum field in the subatomic particle, the aura in the human body, electrostatic layer in the planets and electromagnetic field in the environment; they are layers of energy surrounding every physical body and record all the emotions that have been produced around it. It later on uses this information to influence anybody that comes into contact with this specific body."

– "Excuse me." I said in order to let him know I had barely understood his words. "Could you please give me some examples that will help shed more light on these subjects? They are so foreign and the information is so new that I am confused as to what you are saying."

– "Everything is energy and that energy comes from the ethers. You already know that energy cannot be destroyed, only transformed; human beings continually transform energy with every thought we have, every word we speak, everything we feel and do, and the way we nourish ourselves physically, mentally and spiritually. Every atom has a magnetic field which protects it and records everything that is perceived; for humans, this is what is called *the aura*; for the planets, it is called *electrostatic layers*; for the minerals, vegetables and animals, it is called *the auric egg* or *electromagnetic energy*. Everything you think, speak and feel is recorded in your auric field, the energy field that surrounds you and which in turn takes what it records and impregnates with it every place you visit or go through, the clothes you wear and the people you relate with; in the same manner, that auric field gets impregnated by the energy recorded in the places you visit and by the thoughts, words and feelings of the people that you share with. The process runs both ways.

I will give you several examples to clarify the concept and its impact in our lives: let us assume you had a very sad and depressed day; your plans did not materialize as you wanted them to. You come back home and, although you are not conscious of it, the walls of your house begin to get soaked by your emotions; if these are recurring emotions, in time, the mere fact of coming back home will unconsciously generate in you the feelings of poverty and depression, as a result, you will reject your home and will desire to spend more time in other places. Even more, if you do not wash your clothes, when you put them back on you will attract the same sensations into your life."

– "That is very bad!" I exclaimed. 'What can we do? What is the solution? Generally speaking, we bring home all our problems and we re-live them when we talk about them with our family, and we kind of do it as a way to lighten the load."

— "That is true; but when you have this information you focus on talking about solutions. If you had a bad day, take a shower and wash your clothes as soon as you get back home. Do your best to not fight at home. Try to keep all thoughts about lack, sickness and any other unpleasant things out of your house; do not live them at home. If you cannot help it, clean your house's energies by lightning up a candle, opening windows, keeping live flowers inside, filling the house with light, good thoughts and prayers. The day you go through hardships, those positive energy fields will comfort you. When you enter a place where there was much suffering, you will get soaked in it and attract it into your life; also, when you move to a place where there was much lack, sickness and conflicts, your existence gets disrupted and perturbed and you do not even know why."

— "Is that the reason we feel so good when we wear or use something new for the first time, like clothes, a car, a house or a bed?"

— "Yes, that is the reason. At that moment the energy of the object is pure, it has no programs and you can program it with whatever you desire. Let your body be a temple; put away the demons of doubt and anything that causes you to feel unhappy; do the same with your house and workplace. Pay attention to the places you frequent in your life and the people that you share with, making sure they are filled with good vibrations so they can have a positive impact in your life."

— "It seems to be very important to put all of this information into practice. I must move from the theory into action."

THE ACTION

A lot of times people fill their minds with information, and in some cases, they find the right answers and solutions, but only to others, because in their lives everything remains the same. The best way to find things already made is to make them happen now. It may have happened to you that sometimes you come across people whose results are not the ones you wish to model, however, they let you know they have all the information you need in order to change your life. Undoubtedly, the question to ask in this case is this: *Why don't they change their life first?* Jesus Christ already gave us the lesson: 'By their fruit you will recognize them.' This is the difference between a master and a teacher; the teacher teaches theory, while the master teaches by example.

Action is the mother of wisdom because we only gain experience through action, and when we have experiences we are living and leaving a legacy that will be recorded in the collective unconscious.

Some things to consider with regards to what to do are the following:

- Action heals fear.
- To have a clear picture of the successful result, vividly imagined in your mind, will stimulate you to spring into action more quickly.
- Actions make you the master of the specific area in which you are performing the action.
- Only applied knowledge persists in the spirit.
- The longest walk begins with one step.
- Real power lies in taking action at the right moment.
- Action is the key to every human realization.
- The end of all knowledge is to lead you into action.
- The present is the moment of power; begin taking action now.
- Every coherent decision is followed by immediate action.
- It is only different actions which lead to different results.
- Confirm that each action you take leads you to the successful result that you have chosen.
- To delay action is to betray your dreams, and as such, your own self.
- Action is to be taken now, not at any other moment, it is right here in this place and no other.

- Life is movement; when you stop moving you begin to die.
- Do every one of your pending chores right now.

– "At first sight, each one of these considerations seems very simple and obvious to follow." I said.

– "I know. Although life, in and of itself is very simple, it is us humans who constantly try to make it complicated through theories that lead us into long and tedious analysis processes; this in turn keeps us continuously paralyzed. Mastery comes from uninterrupted action, and this is something humanity values very little these days. For the most part, it is best to make a mistake through action - because at least we obtain mastery on how not to do something - rather than to allow ourselves to be tempted by inaction. Some time ago, someone asked the scientist and inventor Thomas Alva Edison how he felt about the fact he had failed about five to ten thousand times before he was ever able to come up with the light bulb. His answer was this: 'I learned about five to ten thousand ways in which not to make a light bulb.'

The road of success does not put **action** in the first place because that is not its place. I insist, the first and main thing is to know exactly what you want, then you choose the information, you pay attention to viruses that may be thrown your way, you have the right beliefs, choose the attitude that empowers you to display the right kind of behavior and physical memory, and then take action. What this means is that if you follow all the steps correctly, the action will surely happen by itself, and even better, it will a proper and focused action.

Michael Jordan, the great American basketball player, wrote in his book 'I can't accept not trying' the following: *You can practice shooting eight hours a day, but if your technique is wrong, then all you become is very good at shooting the wrong way.*

If you have followed correctly the road of success, you must conquer yourself in order to take immediate action; only then you will be ready to do things right, knowing exactly what you want, that is, your deepest desires. When you find yourself thinking too much before taking action, block the thought by getting into action right away; when you know what you want to do you do not need to think, you only act. After following correctly the road of success and arriving at the stage of getting into action, you only need to act, not think, because at that moment those who think lose."

– "The one who thinks losses?" I repeated.

– "Yes. I will explain it better; when you choose between going to the gym to improve your physical body or staying home watching your favorite show or sleeping, your emotions will guide you to whichever gives you the most pleasure. Remember, the mind is designed to increase pleasure and/or avoid pain, as a result, and given the choice, it will try to keep you from going through the uncomfortable task of getting up from bed and will keep you focused on the pleasure you feel by lying there; it will also make you feel lazy and like you do not even want to make the effort or go through the trouble of exercising. So, before the thought even comes to you, it is best to just get up and go work out; allow your mind to show you only the pleasure that you will feel of being in top physical shape. The same thing happens between listening to the radio or to a self-development audio CD; you must immediately spring into action and listen to the CD; otherwise, you will find every single reason why you should listen to your favorite radio station.

Once you follow every single step on the road of success, take immediate action; become a master of action because that is what makes the difference, no matter how much you fail. The worse mistake you can make is not to act. Whenever you find yourself blocked, like you cannot take action, check yourself because maybe you are being too analytical; you might be in a state of paralysis by analysis. Our internal dialogues hold the key to our state of action or paralysis. Tell yourself whatever is necessary in order for you to spring into immediate action. It is best to sleep tired than frustrated. There are many gifted people who are a failure because they have a bad habit of not taking enough action or do not take it in the right moment."

– "When and how do I know something is not good for me, and that I must stop doing it so I do not become stubborn?"

– "That is an interesting question. You must determine it in the first step on the road of success, at the moment you establish your successful result. The moment you have a clear image of the ecology of your dream - meaning your dream is good for you and the whole of humanity - or what we call the greater good, and then you followed the road of success step by step, then there is no excuse for you to not keep trying. Remember: the winner is the one who never gives up until the end. Losing time is such a waste for the whole of humanity, and it is an indication that we need to forge our character to take immediate action. We must learn that perseverance and persistence are our great helpers in the conquest of your dreams. When you choose to never give up, no matter what happens, and that you will not stop until you achieve your successful result and then you are coherent with this decision, you are being perseverant; and when you make every moment of your life count toward the achievement of that dream, you are being persistent; and so it is that the one cannot work without the other, which means you need to be perseverant and persistent.

Decisions must be renewed on a daily basis. Some time ago, I heard that the best decision only lasts three days; as a result, you must fill yourself with reasons to renew your desire to act toward the conquest of your goal on a day to day basis. If you try it and fail you have the option to try again and learn from your mistake; if you do not act, then you have learned nothing. The message is this: act with perseverance and persistence in order for your dreams to manifest as fast as you deserve."

– "Now I understand that people prefer to give up rather than to persevere because giving up appears to be easier, even though their self-esteem and self-image may begin to wither as a result of those seemingly insignificant but powerful actions."

– "Well said, now you are beginning to understand that it is not about making big changes, but small ones. Most of the people do not know the value of small changes, ignoring they hold the key to our destiny. Small changes in the way we act now will put us in a much different place in the destiny of our future. **Action** is a relationship between the price to pay and the prize. If the price is too high, a wise part of yours that loves to win will push you toward inaction. Make sure your prizes motivate you enough to make it worth it to pay the price, this way you will always find yourself taking proper action.

Wisdom comes when information transforms into experiences through action. That may be the reason you came to this world, to create edifying experiences; in other words, to live, because only when you experience do you really live. Allow for edifying experiences to fill your everyday. Many people go around having ground hog days because somehow they made a habit out of not wanting to have new experiences through action, so they stay stuck in the information stage. Every day must be filled with the magic of the new; you need to open up to the expectation of waiting for life today to be beautifully different.

I repeat, you cannot live for real without action; without it, all you do is vegetate. Do not allow your memory to condemn you to living a ground hog day. Even though the calendar says it is Monday, or Tuesday or Wednesday again, or January, February or whatever month of the year, it has nothing to do with the previous Monday or the previous month of January; this moment is new, it did not exist before and it will not repeat itself ever again, so make it new. Live every moment of your life, not as if it was the last, but like it is the only one. Make every moment count and occupy yourself with the business of being happy, continually asking yourself this: what must I do in order to be happy... and then do it."

– "And everything is allowed? I could do anything I desire in order to create new experiences regardless of how much good or bad I do to others?"

– "The Universe responds to a set of immutable laws that, whether you know about them or not, rule our destiny and are in charge of taking you along the path of the greater good and the highest of ends."

– "What are these rules?"

– "I will name two of them: the law of reversibility and the law of cycles."

– "Would you please explain them to me?"

– "The law of reversibility drives a every person to repeat the same lesson, over and over until it is fully learned; at that moment the person is ready to have a different experience. This law also applies when a person causes harm to another one: the harmful action returns to the originator so the person can experience it in the flesh, and then decide whether it is something he likes to attract into his life or not. The law of reversibility is in charge of giving back a similar experience until the day the person stops doing what he does not want done unto him. A proper question to ask yourself during a crisis is this: What do I need to learn from this experience?

The law of cycles is pretty self-evident. If you pay close attention, you will observe that life repeats itself constantly: Sunday, Monday, Tuesday, Wednesday, and so the week goes; January, February, March, and the rest of the year until it starts again; the same happens with the seasons of the year, day and night, etc. You can read books on astrology and find out that the cycles of every planet repeat themselves; the Earth makes a full revolution around the sun every 365 and a quarter of a day, and one revolution on its own axis every 24 hours, eternally. Life is cyclic, and if the person does not wake up, time will pass by his existence and he will grow old, and nothing more will have happened. You may stop sharing with a certain person in your life, and several years may go by, but when you see this person again and interact with him, you notice, to your surprise, he is still going through the same kind of problems, same excuses and getting the same kind of result, just as if time has never gone by. The antidote for this situation is to cut ties, make changes; remember, people who tell you they wish to change but continue to do the same thing every day suffer from one of the most common illnesses: self-deceit. Do not listen to what people say, but look at what they do, and then you will see if they are really changing direction or simply doing the same thing with their lives, in which case they will continue to get the same results.

What harms humanity is not action, but inaction out of fear to make mistakes, for when you act you experience how to obtain - or not - the result that you want. We harm ourselves the most when we are inactive, when laziness begins to be a part of our daily life and our mind begins to act like a wild buck, out of control, flooding our mind with thoughts that fill us with darkness and vice instead of bringing light into our existence. The game of life is very simple: either you live your purpose or you live in vice; we will talk more about this later.

People give up very easily, becoming quickly inactive out of fear to make a mistake and fail, forgetting that action already carries within itself the reward of experience. Every time you set a goal for yourself, almost immediately appears an obstacle as big as the goal itself; the obstacle is trying to get the eternal established within you, things that will always be of help to you, lessons like determination, courage, perseverance and discipline. Many people live their lives desiring to be free; however, they enslave themselves through their actions, forgetting that only discipline sets them free. Because of this, either you become disciplined by your own volition or go find someone who will instill discipline in you. Discipline is to take immediate action. Ask yourself this: what action must you take right now that will lead you to the realization of your dreams, to the achievement of the successful result you wish to create?

Remember, to postpone action is to betray your dreams, and with that, your own self. Focus on the benefits of taking action now; in your mind, continually celebrate the result you so desire as if you already have it and that will support your decision to act. The best way to conquer you is to make a list of the things you commit to doing every day and avoid going to bed without having done each one of them. It is best to commit to doing fewer things and accomplish them all, rather than committing to doing much and not being able to do them all.

- ❖ Take action and get up at the hour you established the day before; just do it, do not think, act and get up at that time of the day.

- ❖ Take action and begin your day with a prayer and putting yourself in the light, so that everything that happens to you throughout the day will be for your greater good.

- ❖ Take action and look at your vision board before you got to bed and after you get up.

- ❖ Take action and say your decrees or affirmations when you determine that you will.

- ❖ Take action and visualize your dreams until they materialize.

- ❖ Take action and invoke the light during every important moment of your life, to separate the light from the darkness and that only the good comes to you.

- ❖ Take action and only read information that leads you to the conquest of your successful results.

- ❖ Take action and choose what to listen to, and be more prepared with each passing day.

- ❖ Take action and eat properly, and exercise in whatever way is necessary in order to stay in shape.

- ❖ Take action and make the most of every moment of your existence and relate to the right kind of people, meaning, those who know how to get what they want because they either already did it, or are where you want to be, or are on their way.

- ❖ Take action and give thanks when you go to bed for the events and means you used during the journey of the day; do not go over the way the day went, but how you wished it would have been.

- ❖ Take the decision to act because therein lies the experience, which in turn leads you to wisdom. You can compile theories from books, but the experience is the only thing that adds value to your life.

❖ Take action. To be responsible is to have the ability to answer promptly to the tasks we have self-imposed.

If you find yourself paralyzed at any given moment, it probably means that you are focusing on the process, reviewing what it will cost you to achieve what you want. Since you already know it is more important to get the result rather than to be right, take your thoughts back quickly to the successful result; this will fill you up with all the energy you need to prompt you into action. Life is an illusion, in which everything, including your body, will transform. It is more convenient to work for the eternal things, so the real conquest lies in conquering our own selves. More important than to do something is to take action at the right moment, the internal conquests, to become the owner of our own destiny, to be the creator of our future.

When you say that you are going to do something and you do it, your self-esteem and self-image improve and so does your self-worth, self-love and self-assurance; you become more secure with yourself. On the other hand, every time you tell yourself you are going to do something and you do not do it or delay it, you will realize that you will feel drained of your energies and your inner dialogues will say something like this: I am not worthy, I am good for nothing, I am a fraud, I am not important. Because of this, it would be convenient for you to commit to yourself and to others only when you are sure that no matter what you will fulfill your promise at the right moment. Do not forget that mediocre people hide behind excuses. To do away with the excuses is to conquer ourselves.

Focus is one of the keys to taking action; you must learn to differentiate between direct actions, indirect actions, time thieves and mental viruses. Let us analyze these concepts.

Verify the area of your life that you desire to focus your action on and the specific result that you desire.

Let us assume you want to earn a certain amount of money on a monthly basis, and let us perform the analysis assuming that the way you generate your income is by selling a certain product. Review the actions you have been taking on a daily basis and determine the what type they are: if the action leads you directly or indirectly to the conquest of your goal or maybe it takes you farther away from it or robs you of your time. The ones you need to focus on, if you really want to achieve your objective, would be the direct actions; and these are, among other things, to make a list of potential buyers, call them, let them know the benefits and specifications of your product and then close the sale.

Indirect actions make you more effective, and they are the ones you should spend the less time focusing on even though they are also important. Some of these are: become knowledgeable on the products and your company, learn some principles of success and learn to relate correctly with your clients. You can achieve all of these by means of taking a live, book or CD-based training program. Without indirect actions, you could fall in the trap of being active but not productive.

Time thieves are actions that do not lead you to the conquest of your dreams, and you should not dedicate much time to these. In terms of the current example, spending time learning another language would be a time thieve. Although it is convenient to know another language, it will not lead you to the conquest of your successful result which is to earn a certain amount of money per month. Now, it would be a completely different story if you had goals that involved getting into the international world of commerce; at that moment, to learn another language would be a very convenient and direct action. It all depends on what your successful result is.

Some people sacrifice the desire to do something they like while working toward achieving a certain goal, and this they call a *delayed gratification*. It is an effective procedure that helps you to take action in the right moment. If you like to smoke and you commit to doing it only after you have accomplished a certain objective, it is very likely that your basic self, the part of you that supports action, will support you to act on and be constant about it in order to reach your objective, quicker than you would otherwise, just so you can take your prize.

Mental viruses are all of those thoughts that sabotage and take you away from the conquest of your dream, making you feel not worthy of achieving it. To think that in order to earn that money you should be more attractive or intelligent, or that you need to be more cultured or belong to a better family; either one of these will turn into a virus that will keep you from achieving your results. Observe these viruses and eliminate them through the practice of self-acceptance and re-framing your inner dialogues. Remember, a powerful antivirus is to say this to you: *I deserve the best, prosperity and unlimited success just as I am.*

If you want to spend most of your time taking direct actions, the ones that will really take you to the conquest of your dream, turn your wishes into needs. Only when you turn your wishes into needs do you apply another very effective principle of action, and that is the *sense of urgency."*

– "Mr. Deeb," I interrupted, "how do we turn our wishes into needs?"

– "A need is something very urgent that cannot be delayed; an action that must be performed immediately and without which it is impossible to continue to live, such as breathing. Imagine that the life of the person you love the most depends on the conquest of a certain objective, and if you do not accomplish it at the appointed day and time, that person will die; what would you do? When would you begin to act? Or maybe you desire to go to the bathroom because you have a terrible stomach ache; when will you go? Turn your desires into requirements and convince yourself that you cannot live without achieving them.

Do everything you need to in order to take action NOW! If you are planning to take action you might be deceiving yourself; just do it. Take the decision of doing what you need to do, right now. Only when you perform different actions will you obtain different results. When the action is consistent you get continually closer to your results; the universe supports unconditionally those who are determined to make their dreams come true.

Record it in your mind. Let your life always be filled with movement and focused action; know that you are living and that inaction is a way of dying in life and killing your dreams. One thousand daily affirmations for the course of forty days will seal a creation; after that period of time, you do not need to repeat it any longer. You asked me why that number of repetitions and no other, any why that amount of time and no other. The answer I gave you had a lot to do with forging character and educating the inner narrator. I know that all it takes is one affirmation for you to create your reality just like that. But I also know that if you focus on saying your thousand affirmations during the course of forty days, the following two things will happen: that inner narrator of tales, the little voice that tends to constantly take your attention away and rob you of your energy without you even noticing, it will begin to lose its power over you as it becomes educated. As a result, you will become more in charge of your inner dialogues. Also, your character is built as it becomes stronger, and no matter the circumstances you will persevere until the end. You already know that all decrees work regardless of how many you have, but once you seal your creation, you free yourself from being attached to the outcome.

Remember the answers you may get when you ask God for something: '*You want this? Take it;*' another one is '*You will get what you want later, not now*' because it may be convenient for you to learn a certain lesson before you get it, and the last one could be '*You will not get what you want because I have something better in store for you.*'

Some very knowledgeable people affirm that when you die, your achievements will be directly proportional to your capacity to have done what you should have in life beyond circumstances, and to your capacity to turn into the person you always dreamed of being; we are never given a dream for which we do not have the ability within to realize it. People who are afraid of success are used to getting committed with others, as well as with themselves, and to setting such high goals that when they do not fulfill them they have the perfect excuse to justify their failure. They reason that others, under similar circumstances, would probably fail as well to obtain the results; this in turn diminishes the pain they experience as a result of their failure. I hope you do not play those games because it is not good for you. Set goals for yourself that are high enough to motivate and put you into action, with the certainty that they are possible to attain rather than a sabotaging source of distraction."

– "How do I know if my goals are too high?"

– "That is an excellent question with an extraordinarily simple answer. Set goals that are as high as you desire them to be in order for you to feel enthusiastic about them, but only for as long as they invite you to get into action. If a certain goal is set so high up above that you do not want to spring into action, re-think and re-set that tendency to self-sabotage. Remember, the key lies in action. A question you must ask yourself when you find yourself inactive is this: *why not now?* And this other one is a question that will help you to jump into action immediately: *How would I benefit from taking action now?* Or this one: *How will it affect me to not take action now and how will it impact my future?* By the way, it is good for you to know there are correct and incorrect questions."

– "I would tend to think all questions are correct but the answers can be incorrect" I said.

– "The answers that you are looking for are all inside of you and in the macrocosm with all its wisdom. What you need is to connect with the proper stream of information by means of asking the right question. To consciously realize that all the answers you seek already exist, and that to ask the right question will lead to the right answer, and vice versa, is a great step to take on the road to conquering your successful results. If you ask the questions, *what am I doing wrong? Why can't I get the results I want?* Many answers will come from within you telling you all sorts of things to make you feel guilty; *you must be doing many things wrong since you are not getting the results you want.* However, those questions will not add anything significant to your life, all they do is debilitate you. It is a very different thing if you formulate the right kind of question, such as: *What must I do to improve this situation?* Or, *what must I do in order to obtain the result I want?* These new questions will bring forth a better type of information that will truly help you arrive faster to the place you wish to go to or get the prize you desire so much.

Just as an example, let us make a list of some very empowering questions and some that are not. Following some of the principles of success that you have learned so far, let us formulate first the incorrect ones. Remember, we first talk about our mistakes and then about what we are doing right; first about our past and then about the present and the future. Your focus, in the end, just as the last thought to go to bed with, must be on the prize, the successful result, the desired future, all you did right during the day because as you remember from some of our previous meetings, that is the raw material with which to build your next thoughts, and your thoughts create images which in turn create the reality of your world.

Disempowering questions:

What am I doing wrong?
What was my mistake?
How can you have so much debt?
Why can't you achieve what you want?
Why didn't you submit the report on time?
Why didn't you come to the meeting?
Where am I missing the point?
Why do I have this sickness?

The key to determining if a question is incorrect is to observe where the answer leads you: if it leads you to justify why you cannot achieve your goal, to make excuses or focus on the negative, it most certainly is an incorrect question.

Empowering questions:

What must I do in order to accomplish my objective?

How did you do such a successful job?

What would I like to have a year from now?

What would I like to be a year from now?

How would I like to be a year from now?

Why do I want to do this job?

Why do I want to work out an hour a day?

What do I need to learn from this situation?

What is the cure for my sickness?

What is my purpose on this day?

Who are the important people in my life?

What do I need to do in order to be the best in my class?

What do I need to do in order to finish all my assignments today?

Where should I start in order to achieve my goals?

– "The key to know if a question is the correct one is to observe whether it leads you to the successful result or not, whether it focuses you on acting and in the positive aspects of it." He looked at his watch and as if remembering he had something else to do, said, "Habits, we will talk about them tomorrow. I must leave now; I will see you tomorrow at 11 in the morning. Can you be here at that time?" And he got up from the couch without saying another word.

– "Yes, Mr. Deeb," I said affirmatively while at the same time thinking that no matter at what time he would ask me to be there, I would meet him for sure. Without thinking about it twice, I got up from the chair and thanked him for his time.

I left the office perplexed. I wanted to continue to enjoy his teachings, but I understood that once again he was instructing me with his example: that when we have the right kind of information all we need is to do is act, rather than to think. Maybe he left because he remembered he had something important and urgent to do and chose not to be occupied with anything else, instead, he sprung into action immediately and that is mastery. The night went by at the speed of life; my inner narrator played with my mind by filling me with fantasies which made me feel special, lucky and committed to my future; my thought focused on taking immediate action as soon as I knew of something I had left unfinished.

The next day I woke up very early and like on previous occasions I was ready for my interview way in advance. I arrived an hour early and took advantage of it to continue to read a book I had begun quite a while ago and had never finished. I remember I read somewhere that only ten percent of the people who buy a book, read it all the way to the end, so my intention was to begin our meeting with that question. After all the protocol of saying our hellos and asking each other how everything was and how we felt, I began our meeting by asking that question.

– "Mr. Deeb, with regards to the subject of taking action, what must I do if I have too many books I began to read and I have yet to finish?"

– "Take one of the books in your hands and decide whether you really want to finish it or not. If the answer is yes, begin to read it and do not commit to any other material or book until you have finished that one, and then keep going that way until you finish with the last one of those pending. If the answer is no, say out loud, 'I am done with my intention of reading this book, I declare it to be complete and perfect up until the point that I have read so far,' and then forget about it."

– "What is next on the road of success?" I asked, attempting to let him know I did not wish to interrupt him again.

– "Habit," He answered, "we could define them very simply as this: they are actions we have repeated to such an extent that they turned into second nature."

– "What do you mean by second nature?"

– "They are unconsciously learned reactions. It is the way we act under certain circumstances without even noticing. Some scholars on the area of human behavior affirm that any action repeated for a period of twenty-one days will turn into a habit by the end of such period of time. Others say you need to repeat the action for a period of thirty-three days, and others say it takes forty days in order for it to become a real habit."

– "Which one is true?" I asked.

– "You must try it yourself and see if and how it works in your own life, and when the experience gives you a confirmation you will have your own truth. We really are slaves to our habits, and the fact we know we can create whatever habit we desire and turn it into second nature through repetition is excellent news. If we are conditioned by our habits, we might as well do what every person of success does, which is to consciously create the habits that support the achievement of their objectives. Most of the people who fail lack the ability to look at the bad habits that take them to the place they do not want to go to, instead, they tend to blame others for it. These are some of the habits you might want to acquire:

o   Acquire the habit of talking only about positive things, and if you do not have anything good to say you better not speak.
o   Acquire the habit of taking action at the right moment, honoring your commitments and finishing what you start.
o   Acquire the habit of champions by creating a wonderful relationship with God and leaving everything in His hands; act with determination, as if everything depends on you, but trusting that everything is in the hands of God and all your dreams will materialize in the right place and at the right moment.
o   Acquire the habit of living life from the perspective of the observer, eliminating all thoughts of judgment and criticism from your mind; just observe how people live creating through their beliefs and habits, and verify if their results are worthy of you or not so you can choose whether to imitate them or not.
o   Acquire the habit of constancy, determination, perseverance, faith, discipline and honoring your word, meaning, acquire the habit of working continually for the betterment of your own self and to live in the road of excellence.
o   Acquire the habit of being happy and increasing the light in the world; that everywhere you go is left a better place, and that whoever you are with is left a better, happier person after you leave.

Lastly, I would like for you to ponder about the fakir, the monk and the yogi that every human being carries within them: the fakir invites you to conquer the physical body through sacrifice; the monk invites you to conquer your emotions through prayer and meditation; and the yogi invites you to conquer your inner narrator through focus and concentration. Once you master these three aspects, you will recognize that the world is yours and you have to earn it."

– "Mr. Deeb, I would very much like it if you could summarize the road of success." I said timidly.

– "Of course, son, it would be my pleasure; it simply is this:

beliefs + habits = successful results.

Whenever you are creating something, bring your attention to the center of your brain and you will see how your creations will come true faster. Do not get distracted looking for a teacher to follow; whenever you are ready, your level of vibration will bring into your life the people that will take you to the next level, to your next stage in evolution.

Every moment of your existence, you are choosing to live in the law or by grace. In the law, there are losers, guilty people, life is a struggle; lack and difficulty are the order of the day; there is only the chosen one and the rest of the people earn the daily bread by the sweat of the brow. In the grace miracles happen right and left, everything works through love, happiness, the principle of win-win, kindness, the greater good; we become responsible for our creations and our dreams come true very easily.

Every person's name has a meaning; I hope yours means that you are a credible, trustworthy, honest, determined person, with much character and mastery. When the mere thought of the name of a person makes you relate it to the characteristics of the Being, rather than to what the person does or has, that is when you know this person is a being of light.

The most important thing about the road to success is to put it into practice. If you are starving, it is of no use to read the restaurant's menu if you do not order something and eat. The next step is action, remember: action, action, action and then magic happens; miracles will begin to happen in your life more frequently, and you will notice that you are the owner of your destiny and that your deepest dreams are coming true.

These are the lessons I was intending to teach you. With this we put an end to our meetings and my task is concluded, now everything is in your hands; now you will not be able to say that you did not know how, and the only thing you will have is the question whether you are willing to take responsibility for your own future and put all of this information into practice. Be careful and do not try to go out there to change the world with your words; instead, put your effort on turning yourself into an inspiring example worth following. In reality, people do not need to be saved because no soul will ever be lost. No one will thank you for teaching them what you know when they have not asked for it, or for criticizing them because they do not know how to do one thing or another, or because they lack a certain kind of information. People only wish to be loved and accepted as they are, and when you do that, they are willing to change and become energized to take the next step toward their evolution.

Only love heals, only love can teach; only love transforms. Love yourself unconditionally, love others unconditionally and love God and all of His creation unconditionally and you will become a warrior or light.

I feel very happy knowing I have given you this legacy, to know I have shared this information with you. I know that to give it to you was one of the things I came to do in this world, and now I feel I have more energy knowing I have completed one of my pending issues. Because of this, I must thank you and, as always, wish that God may give you His blessings. Remember that you are at home, and I will be very happy to help you in whatever way I can."

— "Thank you, Mr. Deeb." I said, as I searched my mind looking for something else to say, looking for an excuse to continue our meeting and feeling nostalgic at the thought this was the end of it. However, those were my last words, and I left the place feeling a mix of strange feeling; a great sense of happiness to know I had had the privilege to receive so much information, yet sad to know my frequent meeting with Mr. Deeb were over.

It was the middle of the day and a storm lingered in the sky; the sound of thunders reverberated in the distance and a lightning show dominated the horizon. Rain poured down the heavens and my heart shrunk. I wanted to cry and to have the courage to do it; "just as nature did," I thought to myself, but my childhood beliefs won the battle whispering old tales and ill advice at my ear, and it all sounded to me like the typical definition of a regent thought: Men don't cry.

PART SIX

"I would like to perform miracles," said Arthur one day.
"This world exists because of you." Replied Merlin, *"Don't you think that is enough of a miracle?"*
Deepak Chopra (The Way of the Wizard)

REMEMBRANCES

Life went by at top speed and I was barely aware of it. Random events and causalities began to fill my every moment, at the same time that I felt more and more conscious of the way I was achieving my results. I had the good fortune of repeating the workshop on self-knowledge, just as Mr. Deeb had recommended me to do. I took it with one of his most beloved facilitators, Mr. Enrique Leal; then I repeated it over and over again because I felt a powerful inner call to prepare to teach it myself. To share this information with so many people and delivering them from the valley of ignorance in which they are the victims of destiny became a part of the purpose of my life.

In the meanwhile, my life had been turned completely upside down and it appeared this was the price to pay for the privilege of having so much information. It was as if God can never give us new information without also requiring that we put it into practice. My whole world seemed backwards; I had lost my job – a job that in all honesty, I did not like – and my sense of lack at the time made me think I needed to find a new one and depend on it, even if I did not like what I was doing, so I could have the stream of income I needed to exist... better to earn a little but to be sure of it, is what they say. One of the thoughts or paradigms on lack I managed to quickly identify was that concept of working on something we do not like for a wage that is never enough.

My love life was in the same train; a six year relationship went down the drain as well, helping me understand the power of information and how important it is that people who share their lives together should nourish their spirit with the same kind of information. I rented a room in a pension located in one of the most popular barrios of the city; I studied by night and my debts increased by the day. After a short while, and given the results I was getting in life, my spiritual life became broken; I doubted everything and everyone and feeling the experience from all of those workshops and my meetings with Mr. Deeb did not bring enough into my life in order for my experiences to change.

I had all the perfect answers to everyone's problems; I knew exactly how to improve their lives, and the ironic thing was that they did improve. I found that teaching made me feel useful, and the more people learned about these teachings the more I felt I was in the right path. In the meanwhile, Mr. Deeb's words never stopped resonating in my mind: in these times, to teach by example is not an option but a moral obligation, and it is the way to thank God for the good fortune of having the proper kind of information. I was merely one person who had more information than successful results to show for, and for that my ego was out of place, because it presumed of knowing it all and having the right answer to everything, overestimating itself and driving most of the people I knew away from me. So in order to not feel the pain of rejection, I turned into a loner; I wound up with no friends.

Without going into too much detail, that was pretty much the way my life looked like at the time. Then, I did something for my future that was like parting the waters: I began to put Mr. Deeb's teachings into practice. I picked and chose from the information that came into my life and kept taking self-improvement workshops, as well as everything related with self-knowledge and how to be a better person. I practiced my decrees and affirmations with discipline and began to be surprised by how fast I was getting results. A few years later I began to teach the self-knowledge workshop at some of the jails in the city, and I also created two more workshops of my own. Little by little, my life began to transform and the winds began to blow in my favor.

At the beginning of the 1990's, on a day that was September 18th, Mr. Deeb left this planet. On the next day, September 19th (the same day my first son would be born fifteen years later), thousands of people showed up to his funeral in order to express their gratitude for the profound positive impact that he had had on their lives.

I personally chose to spend the day teaching one of the workshops in jail. I did not want to disappoint the inmates who felt so eager to learn, for that is what my absence would have done. Ultimately, I felt very proud of my decision, and since I had already learned that people do not die but merely change vehicle, I looked at the sky before I began the class in order to send him light and my deepest thanks for the impact he had had in my life. I sent him light all the way and into eternity in order to connect with him wherever he was, and at that moment I saw his face in the classroom ceiling surrounded by angels. He was present! He had come to say goodbye! Through my feelings I was able to perceive he had approved of my decision to go and teach that workshop instead of going to the funeral, and I understood we are all just passengers of this story called life and that some people we must encounter over and over again.

I remembered the words contained in the book *Jonathan Livingston Seagull* by Richard Bach: 'If our friendship depends on such things as time and space, then when we finally overcome space and time, we've destroyed our own brotherhood! But overcome space, and all we have left is Here. Overcome time, and all we have left is Now. And in the middle of Here and Now, don't you think that we might see each other once or twice?'

That was the last contact I had with Mr. Deeb. Maybe our relationship was one whose beginning I could not remember, yet hopefully we would encounter one another multiple times. That experience was followed by an even more impactful one: I had a dream that I was dead and, not only was I compelled but required to write a book about the revelation I had had in the dream. I was even told the name of the book: *When is too late to love*. Although the marketing geniuses did not approve of the title, I held on to the information I was given in the dream and followed the instructions. Most of the people would think, just by reading the title, that it is some sort of romantic novel and would probably have the tendency to twist the reality of what was written. The reader, though, finds himself in the presence of a manual in human excellence that, if applied by every person, would undoubtedly improve the results they get in life.

Today, two decades after having been blessed by my first encounter with Mr. Deeb, it is a very difficult task to try and remember my past. I remember those days as a time in which I was very ignorant about life and the art of getting successful results, and it makes me wonder how many could improve the quality of their lives by simply applying a few basic principles of success.

I ended up determining the purpose of my life as this: to create spiritual, mental and material wealth for myself and my universe through the discovery and teaching of the love, power and light that we all carry within ourselves. I had understood that poverty is a disease that happens as a result of ignorance, and it was my purpose to erase this ignorance from my life and my environment. Never again did I mistake humility with poverty. I knew that to be rich but humble was better than any other combination that justifies being poor.

My life has changed since then: I graduated as a Public Accountant from a prestigious university in my country; I took several master's degrees in the area of human development and I finished my career as a commercial manager for a transnational company in communications. I had owned several houses already, as well as cars, and I certainly improved the level of comfort in my life. Thank God, my lifestyle kept only getting better and better. I never went back to work just for money, and I even got many things for free. I only did the things I liked and that were in alignment with my purpose, and every day I felt the universe provided me with more than I could ever need.

I had written a book that was selling very well in different countries; I was going around North America, Central America, South America and Europe giving seminars on the principles of success.

Thank God, I met the person who would become my wife. After ten years of marriage, God gave us our first son and we live in a blessed home. We have an ever growing group of friends and among them I recognize some very special beings; I also make sure they apply correct principles in their lives because of the impact they have in the association.

Spiritually speaking, I chose that more than following a specific religion, I preferred living a practical spirituality that brings me ever closer to God. I make a constant effort to live in His light because it brings me an extraordinary sense of security, direction, and purpose in life.

What a simple kind of life! Though it can be turned into something very complicated by people who are incapable of doing what it takes to conquer their dreams; they lose their time in senseless arguments about what is right or wrong.
Since those days, more people have made an impression in my life and nowadays they represent some of the basic pillars supporting who I have become today, whether it may seem like too much or too little to someone looking from the outside. Nonetheless, it is Mr. Deeb who holds a very special place in my life because of the impact of his lessons and wise counsel in the awakening of my consciousness.

"Define exactly what you want," is what he used to say; "choose the information that will support the materialization of your dreams; do not listen to people who say what you want is impossible, it cannot be done or it will not work; work hard as if it all depends on you, and trust that all is in the hands of God. wait with the patience – peace and science – that comes from the wisdom of faith and trusting your wishes will materialize at the right place and time; never allow your anxiety or lack of knowingness to get in between you and your creation; the winner is the one who tries until the end."

To this day, only one question continues to linger in my mind. My body trembles and I thank God profusely every time I think about it...What would my life be if I had never met Mr. Deeb?...

ABOUT THE AUTHOR

DANIEL HERNANDEZ OSORIO

Considered one of the most renowned Latin American speakers in the area of self-improvement, Daniel Hernandez Osorio is a public accountant graduated from the *Pontificia Universidad Javeriana of Bogotá*, Colombia, where he has been teaching Excellence Models. Schooled in Santiago de Chile as master and trainer in Neuro-linguistic Programming. He took the series of seminars "Insight" levels I – IV recognized by the *University of Santa Monica* in California, USA.

A professional in Rebirthing, Creative Thought and Cellular Programming from the *Rebirthing Association of Spain*. He took courses in PhotoReading, Activating your Success, and Mind Mapping from the *Colegio de Investigación y Desarrollo Empresarial* in Mexico.

Mr. Hernandez Osorio has received training in several self-knowledge techniques: Psychodrama, Enneagram, Gestalt, Music Therapy, Hypnosis, Reiki, Mental Power, Macrobiotics, Catharsis, Transcendental Meditation, and Action and Project Management.

He was a radio host and T.V. and radio producer.

Teaches leadership, creativity and communication with emphasis on personal responsibility at several Colombian prisons, as part of his social labor.

Worked in the rehabilitation of combat wounded military personal for the health battalion in Bogotá, Colombia.

Mr. Hernandez Osorio is a successful businessperson in the building of consumer communities or networking. His ample knowledge in the subject has allowed him to train many business employees in several countries around the world. He is the President of the Colombian branch of a distinguished company in the world of Interactive Commerce training.

Noted business consultant for various Latin American companies, he trains professionals in all areas in the principles of success, whom are able to verify the efficacy of what they learn through the undeniable improvement in the quality of their lives, as well as their businesses.

Daniel Hernandez is the creator of three powerful series of seminars in the area of personal development. These are:

1. Self-Knowledge

2. To be born to Love

3. Excellence Models

The seminars are aimed at providing individuals with the tools to better know themselves, to recognize and transform their personal limitations; to learn and to apply principles of success in their lives.

The author invites you to immerse yourself in his books, *When it's too late for love* and *To fail or to succeed: It's your choice* a compilation of principles of success that, not only will it captivate you, but will inspire you to persevere and do whatever it takes in order for you to conquer your dreams, with clarity on your objectives and inner strength.

A NOTE FROM THE AUTHOR

My dearest friend: Do you think this book has provided you with a set of valid tools which will allow you to improve the quality of your life? Did it increase your light? Share it with your friends...

If you wish to participate in one of my workshops or acquire some of our audio, you may contact us via email: daniel.hernandezx1@gmail.com

Visit us on:
https://www.facebook.com/danielhernandezx1

https://www.facebook.com/cuandoparaamarestarde

https://www.facebook.com/fracasarotriunfartueleccion

TWITTER: @DanielHO

Tell me your name, country where you live and the way you came about this book. Any comment or suggestion, you may contact me by email: daniel.hernandezx1@gmail.com

With love and light"

Daniel Hernández Osorio.

Our Publishing commitment: To make available publications that acknowledges, rejoice and promote others to express their true essence. D'har Services Editorial Arte en Diseño Global
www.dharservices.com
Teléfonos 1 877 223 1799 y 786 837 4567

To order all the publications of Daniel Hernández
see: **www.amazon.com**

www.ingramcontent.com/pod-product-compliance
Lightning Source LLC
Chambersburg PA
CBHW062209080426
42734CB00010B/1860